MANNA

MANNA

WHEN YOU'RE OUT OF OPTIONS,
GOD WILL PROVIDE

STEVE FARRAR

NELSON
BOOKS

An Imprint of Thomas Nelson

Published in Nashville, Tennessee, by Nelson Books, an imprint of Thomas Nelson. Nelson Books and Thomas Nelson are registered trademarks of HarperCollins Christian Publishing, Inc.

The author is represented by the literary agency of WordServe Literary Group, www.wordserveliterary.com.

Thomas Nelson titles may be purchased in bulk for educational, business, fund-raising, or sales promotional use. For information, please e-mail SpecialMarkets@ThomasNelson.com.

Interior designed by Lori Lynch.

Any Internet addresses, phone numbers, or company or product information printed in this book are offered as a resource and are not intended in any way to be or to imply an endorsement by Thomas Nelson, nor does Thomas Nelson vouch for the existence, content, or services of these sites, phone numbers, companies, or products beyond the life of this book.

Unless otherwise noted, Scripture quotations are taken from NEW AMERICAN STANDARD BIBLE®. © The Lockman Foundation 1960, 1962, 1963, 1968, 1971, 1972, 1973, 1975, 1977. Used by permission.

Scripture quotations marked KJV are from the King James Version of the Bible.

Scripture quotations marked ESV are taken from The Holy Bible, English Standard Version®, copyright © 2001 by Crossway, a publishing ministry of Good News Publishers. Used by permission. All rights reserved.

Scriptures quotations marked NIV are taken from Scriptures from THE HOLY BIBLE, NEW INTERNATIONAL VERSION®, NIV®. Copyright © 1973, 1978, 1984, 2011 by Biblica, Inc.® Used by permission. All rights reserved worldwide.

Scripture quotations marked NKJV are taken from THE NEW KING JAMES VERSION. © 1982 by Thomas Nelson, Inc. Used by permission. All rights reserved.

Library of Congress Cataloging-in-Publication Data

Farrar, Steve.
  Manna : when you're out of options, God will provide / Steve Farrar.
    pages cm
  Includes bibliographical references.
  ISBN 978-1-4002-0456-4
  1. Providence and government of God--Christianity. 2. Trust in God--Christianity. 3. Faith. I. Title.
  BT135.F375 2016
  231'.5--dc23
                                              2015027213

Printed in the United States of America

16 17 18 19 20 RRD 6 5 4 3 2 1

To my mom,
Beverly Farrar,
for being manna to me
all the days of my life.

CONTENTS

1

EMERGENCIES
AND EXIGENCIES

"It is written: 'Man shall not live by
bread alone, but by every word that
comes from the mouth of God.'"

—MATTHEW 4:4 (ESV)

At some point in your life, you are going to find yourself in a wilderness. You may be there right now as
you're reading this book. There are many kinds of wildernesses: emotional, relational, health, reputation, failure,
unemployment—the list goes on and on.

When you are in the wilderness, you are usually iso-
lated and overwhelmed, and you are cut off from the normal

supply lines of life that keep you going. It is in these times in the wilderness that you find yourself utterly dependent on God for a well-timed help. If He doesn't come through, you're finished.

For forty years, two million men, women, and children were in a holding pattern waiting to go into the land that God had promised them. The historical account is in Exodus 16. These Hebrew families weren't waiting in a city—they were wandering in an extremely rugged and remote wilderness. And God led them there on purpose.

In the wilderness, there was no source of food, so God fed them supernaturally every morning with manna. Manna had never been seen or heard of before. It was a supernatural provision of God that appeared on the ground each morning. The people were instructed to collect only what they needed for each day's provision. If they collected too much, it would rot and grow foul. God designed it this way so that the Israelites would be completely out of food when they went to bed each night. If He didn't come through with the manna the next morning, they would begin to starve. He was forcing these people who doubted Him to learn that He could be trusted to supply everything they needed to survive. All supply lines were cut off in the wilderness. Yet in forty years, not one of these two million ever went hungry. Each day they saw the mighty, supernatural, perfectly timed provision of God.

If you are in some kind of wilderness as you read this book, there is a word that will ring true to you. It is the word *emergency.* My copy of *Webster's Dictionary* defines *emergency* as "a sudden, generally unexpected occurrence or set of circumstances demanding immediate action."[1]

Every night, when the mothers and fathers of Israel put their kids to bed, they were completely out of food. That's what you call an emergency. If the manna, the bread from heaven, wasn't there in the morning, every family in the nation of Israel would be in immediate crisis. But when they got up and went out of their tents, the manna was there, and it was there every time. God never missed in forty years.

Another word you probably don't use too often is *exigency*; the plural is *exigencies.* I mention both the singular and the plural because when you find yourself with one exigency, it almost always causes a chain reaction that burdens you with many exigencies. An exigency is a situation that calls for immediate action and attention. When you have a situation that requires immediate action and attention, other important things are going to have to be put aside and neglected until the exigency can be addressed. Suddenly you find yourself in an emergency of exigencies with pressing needs, pressing demands, and pressing requirements. And the problem is magnified when you look around and find yourself completely out of options. All of the normal supply lines that have always been there to help have been cut off. There is no pressure in the world like that kind of pressure.

What do you need in those situations? You need an immediate help, but it is not within yourself to come up with what is needed. You may be out of cash, out of a job, out of heath care, out of friends, out of family, out of health, out of emotional stability, out of luck, and out of options. You see no possible way out of these crushing and confining circumstances, whatever they may be.

But you are not out of a Savior.

His name is Jesus, and as we shall see, He is your sovereign Defender and Keeper. You may be out of options, but He is never out of anything. He is never out of answers, solutions, or power to immediately come to your aid and rescue you.

In these wilderness times of emergencies and exigencies, He calls us to come to Him just as Hebrews 4:16 describes: "Let us then with confidence draw near to the throne of grace, that we may receive mercy and find grace to help in time of need" (ESV).

John Piper stated that the "traditional translation of Hebrews 4:16 hides from us a very precious promise . . . the Greek original behind the phrase 'grace to help in time of need' would be translated literally, 'grace for a well-timed help.'"[2]

That translation of Hebrews 4:16 has been manna for me for twenty years, and I can still remember the first time I read Piper's insight. I was having a particularly tough day dealing with some financial burdens that were upon me as I was seeking to steward well the openings that had come my way to minister to men. Our ministry was young, but the opportunities were many and the cash flow was minimal. On one particular day in 1993, I was struggling mightily to fight off discouragement. I knew the Lord had called me to do this work among men to help equip them to be spiritual leaders in their homes and churches. I was overwhelmed with the great opportunities that were coming my way in response to my book *Point Man*. But I didn't have the financial resources I needed to fund and hire additional staff. The Lord had obviously called me to this work, and the invitations to speak from churches around the country were pouring in. But I could not handle this all by myself. As the opportunities were growing, the supply lines were rapidly drying up.

As I sat in my study upstairs in our home pondering this most stressful state of events and trying to figure out how to pay the bills that were on my desk, my fax machine suddenly came to life. The cover letter was from one of my editors at Multnomah Books, Steve Halliday. In essence, it said, "Hey, Steve, I'm editing John Piper's new book, *Future Grace*, that will be out next year. As I was working on this chapter, I thought you might find it of interest."

The chapter Steve felt prompted to send to me contained John's observations of Hebrews 4:16. When I read the words "grace for a well-timed help," that was manna to me. In all honesty, I valued those words that day more than I would have a large donation check.

That verse was literally a well-timed help. My financial burden was not lifted immediately, but my spirit was. I knew that the Lord had prompted Steve to fax that to me. He knew nothing of my burden and financial pressure. I hadn't talked to Steve in many weeks. But the fact that the Lord moved him to send one chapter of the book that contained the six words "grace for a well-timed help" meant more to me than I can say.

In reading that chapter, I knew the Lord was letting me know that His eye was upon me and that He had not forgotten me. He knew the pressure I was under. He knew that I was experiencing an emergency and many exigencies. And Piper's words and the verse in Hebrews let me know that help would show up at just the right time.

Did the well-timed help come? Yes, it did, but in all honesty, I cannot remember what it was. But what I have never forgotten is the phrase "a well-timed help." The Lord will come through—not on our time frame, but on His. I survived that crisis, and you will survive yours—and it's all thanks to His manna, the well-timed helps that He tends to send at the last possible moment.

The wilderness is where the Lord does His most important work and His most painful work. When you are in the wilderness, He has your undivided attention. In the wilderness, you've got one thing on your mind: *survival*. When all the supply lines of life that have always been there for you are gone, you don't see any possible way to make it. You're out of options, and you're completely hemmed in. You don't see any way out because there *is* no way out.

But the God of the Bible specializes in making a way *where there is no way*. He can get necessary and immediate provisions to you. He knows who you are, He knows where you are, and He knows more about your situation than you do. His eye is upon you, and although you may feel that He is far off, He is actually very near. Perhaps you are in dire straits that threaten to undo and collapse everything in your life that is valuable. That's the wilderness. The Lord God knows all about it. He knows that you are completely out of options. He understands that you have come to the end of your rope. And to be candid, He prefers that you get to that point. He needs you at the end of your resources so you'll finally think straight about your situation.

Everyone depends on something. But everything, literally everything in the universe, is dependent on God. Why put your dependence on men, or companies, or the stock market, or the price of gold? Why would you depend on anything else than the living God? All things depend upon Him in the first place.

Dependence upon Him is utterly wise and rational, but it usually takes an emergency or crisis to get us to that point. For it is at this point of immediate need that we have no option except to trust Him. That is the place of wisdom, and that is the place of safety. As P. B. Power observed, "God loves trust; it honors Him; he who trusts the most shall sorrow least. If there were continual trust there could be continual peace."[3]

Trust in the living God must be learned over time. We can't get into a microwave, push Trust, and come out three minutes later with continual trust for the rest of our lives. So from time to time He has us revisit the wilderness, and we find ourselves in another emergency that brings along its cousins of exigencies and pressing needs. And once again, we are hemmed in, with no way out, and we have no option except to trust and depend on Him and His promise. This is the real place of thinking straight, for you are now completely dependent upon Him. And in this place, He invites you to call upon Him with your whole heart: "Call upon Me in the day of trouble, I shall rescue you, and you will honor Me" (Ps. 50:15).

He knows how to rescue you in your wilderness.

He knows how to make a way where there is no way.

He knows how to provide a well-timed help just in perfect time.

He proved it every day to two million men, women, and children who wandered in a wilderness for forty years. He never missed a day of faithfully providing what they needed. He was never late, and He was never early. He was always just in time.

MANNA FROM HEAVEN

The issue was starvation. Having been delivered from the bondage of Egypt, God's people found themselves miles upon miles away from any inhabited city. They didn't have time to plant crops because they were on the move. Even if they did plant crops, it would have been a waste of time because the soil was so depleted it couldn't bear crops (Jer.

2:2, 6). It was a wilderness full of deserts and pits and characterized by intense and prolonged droughts. It was a land that no one would dare to cross because it meant certain death. That wilderness, simply put, according to the prophet Jeremiah, was a land "where no man dwelt" (2:6). Mainly, because there was no food. Without food and water, there was no possible way for them to survive in this wilderness, yet they did survive. They had nothing, but they were never without.

There were no markets full of meat, fish, and fresh produce. You don't find markets in a wilderness. There were no Costcos or Sam's Clubs where they could stock up for a month or two in advance. They were completely cut off from any normal sources of food for forty years, but they never missed a meal because He always came through with a well-timed help. Manna was God's supernatural provision that came down from heaven just in the nick of time every single day for forty years. It was a daily, sufficient, constant supply of God's provision. And it told every day of His limitless power and perfect faithfulness.

George Müeller wanted to prove to his generation that God was the living God and that His power was not limited. Müeller was a pastor who lived in England in the 1800s. He looked around the city of Bristol and saw the hundreds of orphans struggling to survive in horrific conditions. The Lord put it on his heart to start an orphanage where these children could be loved, fed, educated, given a trade, and introduced to the gospel of Jesus Christ. But the primary motivation for Müeller was not just to help the orphans. Müeller wanted to prove that it was possible to live off of the promises and faithfulness of God.

In order to prove his heartfelt belief that God would answer prayer and provide according to His promises, Müeller determined never to ask anyone to support the orphanage. He never made appeals, and he never sent out letters asking for donations. He was careful not to judge those ministries who did so, but he knew God was calling him to go about this ministry to orphans in a completely different way. He began with a handful of children, and within a matter of years he was caring for over two thousand orphans who were housed in the orphanage buildings built by donated funds. For sixty years he ran the orphanage without asking anyone for any money.

Believe me, this was no easy task. Müeller found himself in the wilderness of financial and spiritual drought on numerous occasions. But instead of panicking, he prayed. What Müeller did was remarkable. He did not count upon the normal supply lines that most ministries depend on for funding but chose simply to pray and ask God to bring in the daily needs to feed and clothe the orphans and keep the heat on. He recorded it all in his autobiography that sits next to my computer as I type these words. Müeller kept a daily diary of his financial needs, his prayers for God's assistance, and the financial gifts that were given. His records were meticulous. The subtitle of the autobiography of George Müeller is "A Million and a Half Answers to Prayer." The introduction to his book explained, "Without ever asking anyone for help but God alone . . . he humbly claimed that the Lord had answered 50,000 requests, 30,000 of those in the same hour or day in which they were asked."[4]

Now that's what I call well-timed help.

There are times when you will find yourself in the wilderness and you are completely out of what you need. That's when Jesus, who is the Bread of Life, supplies you, His child, with manna. Because Jesus is the Bread of Life on any and every level of your life, I want to offer this broadened definition of manna. Manna is any provision of God in any area of your life that is a well-timed help. Manna is a provision of the Lord Jesus Christ that comes precisely at the right moment.

I have no doubt you have seen Him do this as you look back over your life. Perhaps today you find yourself in a place of crushing pressure. You have a tremendous need, but you are completely out of resources. You see no possible way out of your dilemma. All supply lines have been cut off. You've been thinking you are finished. You remember what happened to you in the past. The Lord came through for you in some unforeseen way and kept you going. Then the inevitable happened. Before long, you encountered another difficulty in the wilderness, and once again you wondered how the Lord would get you through this latest episode.

It seems to me that is the essence of the Christian life. We walk through the wilderness from faith to faith, which is another way of saying from crisis to crisis (Rom. 1:17). The wilderness crises are times of affliction and hardship, and they are a normal part of the Christian life (Phil. 1:29).

There is a reason we keep going through these episodes of testing in the wilderness. Tim Keller summarized it well:

> When pain and suffering come upon us, we finally see not only that we are not in control of our lives but that we never were. . . .
>
> [Suffering] can be an important chapter in our life story and a crucial stage in achieving what we most want in life. But in the strictly secular view, suffering cannot be a good chapter in your life story—only an interruption of it. It can't take you home; it can only keep you from the things you most want in life. In short, in the secular view, suffering always wins. . . .
>
> If you believe in Jesus and our rest in him, then suffering will relate to your character like fire relates to gold. Think of four things that we want. Do you want to know who you are, your strengths and your weaknesses? Do you want to be a compassionate person who skillfully helps people who are hurting? Do you want to have such a profound trust in God that you are fortified against the disappointments of life? Do you want simply to be wise about how life goes? Those are four crucial things to have—but none of them are readily achievable without suffering. There is no way to know who you really are until you are tested. There is no way to really empathize and sympathize with other suffering people unless you

have suffered yourself. There is no way to really learn how to trust in God until you are drowning.[5]

Not long ago I not only thought I was finished but I really thought I was going to die. I felt like I was drowning, and I was utterly exhausted from trying to keep my head above water. The situation was so overwhelming that I truly did not see any way out.

I've been privileged for nearly twenty-five years to minister to men. It has been my great honor to help equip men to become spiritual leaders first in their homes and then in their churches. During those twenty-five years, I have averaged thirty-five weekend conferences a year. I usually write a book about every eighteen months. That means, depending on when you catch me, I'm either researching a book, starting a book, in the middle of a book, or finishing a book. And after a short break, it's time to start the next one. I am so honored to be able to speak and write with a focus on men. But on May 8, 2012, I hit a major wall. And I was scared.

It was a wall of fatigue, exhaustion, and frustration. I was way beyond burned out. I knew in my heart I was about to experience personal internal combustion that was not going to be pretty. I knew I couldn't keep up the travel schedule of thirty-some weekends a year. I needed to cut the amount of trips in half, but I couldn't do that because they kept the ministry funded. I was afraid I was going to drop dead of a heart attack like my brother, Mike, did fifteen years earlier. I was seriously overweight and overworked. I knew I couldn't keep up that pace, but I saw no way out.

On the morning of May 8, 2012, my wife, Mary, and I had a very serious discussion about all of this. She was very worried about me. She had known for years that the pace was too much. We had a very frank conversation about all these factors, and we got down on our knees and asked the Lord to give us clarity and show us what He wanted us to do. Everything was on the table. We asked, "What changes do we need to make, Lord?" As I think back to that morning, the word that comes to my mind is *crisis*. My creative juices were nonexistent. There was nothing left in the tank. I'm not even sure there were any fumes in my tank. I was utterly and absolutely depleted. And I had to get going on another book.

I felt trapped. I had responsibilities and commitments I had made, but I had no energy to get them done. The only other time in my life I had felt this way was in my early thirties. I wound up in a deep depression back then that took me two years to pull out of. And I felt like I was right on the cliff of something like that happening again. That morning as Mary and I prayed, I knew I was in crisis.

Oh, I need to mention another piece of this puzzle. In addition to my traveling, speaking, and writing, I taught a weekly men's Bible study on Wednesday nights at Stonebriar Community Church. Shortly after Chuck Swindoll started Stonebriar, he and his staff asked me if I would be willing to teach a weekly men's study. So we started upstairs in one of the classrooms with maybe fifty or sixty guys. After several months, Jim Gunn, one of the elders, walked in with a small cassette boom box recorder. He asked if I was okay with his recording my message each week. I said sure, so from then on I would teach with a small boom box from Walmart on the table next to me. Over the years, the study continued to grow, and we had to move into larger rooms. At some point Jim ditched the boom box and got some real equipment.

I have been doing the Wednesday night men's study at Stonebriar for fourteen years. The Lord has blessed that work and brings together each week several hundred men to study the Scriptures. Each week the message was recorded and put in a file drawer, and we would make CDs available for guys who wanted them. As the years went by, we received requests for those studies to be made available online. Over the last four to five years, we got e-mails and calls on a daily basis from around the country asking for the men's Bible studies to be online so that the men in their groups could access them.

I knew that was a great idea. Mary had been praying about this for years, and my brother-in-law, Bryan Owens, was also encouraging me in this strategic direction. The problem was that I didn't know how to do that, and I didn't have the funds to hire anyone to take care of it. So I just kept plugging away speaking, traveling, and writing. What I needed to do was to work smarter instead of harder. I needed to travel less and use technology to be more effective in ministry. But I was hemmed in by circumstances I thought were beyond my control, and I couldn't see a way to get out of this quandary.

Let's get back to the morning of May 8, 2012. As Mary and I knelt down to pray, we were completely dependent on the Lord to help us. We had nowhere else to go. But He tells us to come to Him in every situation of life, whether big or small. When we are in trouble and at the end of our ropes, He calls us to come to Him. Psalm 50:15 says, "Call on me in the day of trouble; I will deliver you, and you will honor me" (NIV). And Psalm 142:3 reminds us, "When my spirit was overwhelmed within me, then You knew my path" (NKJV).

When I was overwhelmed and almost out of hope, the Lord knew my path, and He had an answer and solution all set up and ready to go. And He was about to pull back the curtain and show it to us.

Mary and I finished praying that morning, and we had no idea what the Lord was going to do. We just knew that we desperately needed Him to work on our behalf. About thirty minutes later, Bryan called, and the conversation quickly turned to the issue of getting my teaching online. I really didn't want to talk about it, but I couldn't be rude. Bryan asked me how that was going, and I said that I had nothing new to report. I was continuing to get calls and e-mails literally every day, but I had no solution. Bryan then reiterated how critical it was for me to get this in place. "Steve, it's the answer to cutting back your travel and getting your message out to places where you could never go. This is something that has to be done. It would enable you to be a much better steward of your time and energy."

I then asked Bryan what it would cost to take on a project

of converting all of these tapes and CDs from analog to digital. Bryan told me that from his experience it was going to be somewhere in the range of $50,000. And then he said, "Steve, I know you don't do fund-raising for your ministry, but I'm going to pray that the Lord will put this on someone's heart and that this money will come in. This simply has to be done."

I thanked him for his concern and prayers, but I had become a little bit cynical in my own heart. I knew the strategy was a good one, but in spite of Mary's consistent praying, God had not provided a solution, and I began to believe that the Lord was not in it. But His delays are not necessarily His denials, as Obadiah Sedgwick used to say.[6]

I just simply couldn't see how any of this would become a reality. It just seemed way out of the realm of possibility. I was in crisis and needed some immediate help. But as I looked around, I could see no possible way of things changing.

When I got off the phone with Bryan, I walked into the bedroom to change clothes to get on the treadmill. Mary had just left to run some errands and I was in the house by myself. As I walked into the bedroom, I was hit by a wave of utter despair. I stopped, put my head against the highboy dresser, and began to weep. I must admit I was shocked by my tears. But somewhere inside me a pressure valve went off, and in utter desperation I said to the Lord, "If You don't help me, I'm going to die." I knew that if I didn't get some kind of relief, the stress and pressure were going to kill me.

Then I asked the Lord to do something else for me.

"Please stop these men from calling me and e-mailing me about this online stuff. For some reason You have kept this from happening and that's fine. But please stop the calls and e-mails. They are wearing me out. I'm not asking You to make this online stuff happen—maybe it's not what You want to do and I'm okay with that—but I'm asking You to stop all the calls and e-mails. I'm not trying to stir up this interest, but it just keeps coming. Please bring it to a halt."

I was utterly discouraged. I was sixty-two years old and had seen the Lord accomplish some great things in my life. He had done more than I had imagined possible through the hundreds of conferences and the distribution of my books. But in my heart of hearts, I felt like my best days were behind me and everything was getting ready to shut down—including me.

There's a reason I'm going into such detail. I know this all sounds pretty hopeless, but the Lord was about to break through. I didn't know it as I leaned my head against that dresser and wept and prayed, but the Lord was going to change everything in the next twenty-four hours. And the events that would transpire that next day would start a chain reaction that would affect every area of my life—health, ministry, travel, family.

I actually do two men's Bible studies on Wednesday, one at noon for sixty or so businessmen and then the Stonebriar men's study in the evening. As I was walking out of the noon study the next day, two guys were standing on the side-walk. I didn't remember their names, but they were regular attenders. One of the guys said, "Is next week our last week before we take the summer break?" As I kept walking toward my car, I indicated that it was. "How am I going to survive without Bible study over the summer?" he said with a smile. And then he said something that made me stop in my tracks. "Seriously, Steve, I travel back and forth to Europe for my work. How come I can't get any of your stuff on the Internet?" I thought, *Oh no, here we go again.*

"I can't find anything, Steve. I was looking last month when I was in Prague. Isn't your study on Wednesday night recorded?"

"Yes, it is. It's actually not only on audio but it's recorded on video."

He was stunned and replied, "You can't be serious—what do you do with it?"

I told him it all went into the file cabinet with the other fourteen years of CDs.

"You mean all of that is just sitting in a cabinet? Why don't you get it online?" he asked. Before I could respond, he said, "Well, that would be a major project and you don't have time to do it. You would have to get the funding and hire someone to do it."

"That's right," I replied. "And I don't really do any fund-raising."

After several minutes of discussing it, he said, "This really needs to be done. It's a matter of stewardship." And he began to tell me exactly what Mary, Bryan, and my associate, Steve Hutton, had been saying for half a decade. I told him

I had been getting e-mails and urgings from them for a long time. There was no question that it was a stewardship issue and it all made sense, but it just had never come together.

"So how much would it cost to get all of that done?" he asked.

I replied that I didn't ask people to give to our ministry. He said with a smile, "I'm just wondering what the cost would be to pull all of this off so you could steward your ministry more effectively."

I told him that Bryan told me it would be somewhere around $50,000. His friend said that it could actually cost more than that.

He then looked at me and said, "Okay."

I looked at this guy and was a little stunned.

"Okay?" I said. "Okay what?"

He smiled again and said, "Okay, you've got it. I'll cover the cost. And if it turns out to be more than $50,000, I'll make sure it's covered. Now, let's get to work to find someone who can oversee this for you and get this off the ground."

And then out of my mouth came the only words that seemed appropriate: "I'm sorry, but could you tell me your name?" I'm serious. For the life of me I could not recall this guy's name.

In a random and unplanned conversation on a sidewalk twenty-four hours after Mary and I got on our knees, God answered our prayers with a well-timed help. In one conversation, this guy whose name I couldn't remember, wearing a T-shirt, shorts, and flip-flops, committed to write a check to cover the entire cost. And within days the check was delivered. What seemed to be hopeless and completely out of reach was taken care of on a sidewalk as a result of a "chance" conversation. But it was not chance—it was the providence of God. It was His well-timed answer to my desperation.

It was manna.

But the Lord wasn't done. In the next several months, a number of other men, independently of one another, stepped up and began to financially support our work. As a result, I was able to cut my travel in half and actually add some key staff people. This was another well-timed help. If I'm not mistaken, that's what you call manna. It was a remarkable provision of God that enabled what I thought was impossible to become possible. Just five months after praying about the unlikely scenario of cutting my travel in half, the Lord did it. Six months before, I saw no way out of my wilderness. But our God is the God who makes a way when there is no way.

Sometime around Christmas I was standing in the kitchen sipping a cup of coffee. I had lost the excess weight due to a schedule of less travel and more swimming, and I had just been told that men in several countries were accessing our audio and video studies online. Mary walked in and was putting away a few things. She looked over at me and said, "So, how are you doing?" I answered, "I'm doing pretty well." She could tell that I was. And she knew why. I told her, "He's restoring my soul." And it was all because of the provision of God—the well-timed provision of God.

Jesus is the manna.

Jesus is the Bread of Life.

That's why you will make it through your personal wilderness, whatever it might be. If you've ever thought to yourself, *There's no way I'll ever get through this*, then I've written this book for you.

If you've ever looked around and found yourself completely out of options to change your circumstances, then you're the one I hope will read these pages.

His plan for you may be very different from what you have envisioned. Or perhaps it is His timing that you are struggling with, or the deep discouragement that comes from one disappointment after another. These kinds of experiences are common in the wilderness.

Please note that my well-timed help was years in the making. When the answer came, it came like a bullet out of nowhere, but for years it was a matter of simply staying at my post and waiting for God to come through in His time—not mine. Perhaps that's where you are right now. Could it be that you are fighting off the disappointment that comes from waiting on God for a well-timed help?

If so, I give you the wise words of John Newton, which I have quoted before in several other books—but oh, how valuable they are and worth repeating:

> It is indeed natural to us to wish and to plan, and it is merciful in the Lord to disappoint our plans, and to cross our wishes. For we cannot be safe, much less happy, but

in proportion as we are weaned from our own wills, and made simply desirous of being directed by His guidance. This truth (when we are enlightened by His Word) is sufficiently familiar to the judgment; but we seldom learn to reduce it to practice, without being trained awhile in the school of disappointment. The schemes we form look so plausible and convenient, that when they are broken, we are ready to say, What a pity! We try again, and with no better success; we are grieved, and perhaps angry, and plan out another, and so on; at length, in a course of time, experience and observation begin to convince us, that we are not more able than we are worthy to choose aright for ourselves. Then the Lord's invitation to cast our cares upon Him, and His promise to take care of us, appear valuable; and when *we* have done planning, *His* plan in our favour gradually opens, and he does more and better for us than we either ask or think.

I can hardly recollect a single plan of mine, of which I have not since seen reason to be satisfied, that had it taken place in season and circumstance just as I proposed, it would, humanly speaking, have proved my ruin; or at least it would have deprived me of the greater good the Lord had designed for me. We judge of things by their present appearances, but the Lord sees them in their consequences, if we could do so likewise we should be perfectly of His mind; but as we cannot, it is an unspeakable mercy that He will manage for us, whether we are pleased with His management or not; and it is spoken of as one of His heaviest judgments, when He gives any person or people up to the way of their own hearts, and to walk after their own counsels.[7]

2

JESUS IS THE MANNA

"I am the bread of life; he who comes
to Me will not hunger, and he who
believes in Me will never thirst."

—JOHN 6:35

I have an old beat-up and marked-up copy of Thomas Watson's *All Things for Good*, which I read often. Somehow I misplaced it weeks ago and had been hoping it would turn up. I finally came across it. Watson penned this book back in 1663. It is brief but weighty and never fails to yield manna. I just took a minute or two to flip carefully through the pages that could use some Scotch tape on the binding. As I did so, I saw a verse Watson referenced that immediately struck me. The verse is Job 22:21, and Watson rendered it, "Acquaint now thyself with God, and be at peace, thereby good shall come unto thee."

In this chapter I want to give you four principles that will better acquaint you with God, the Father, and His Son, the Lord Jesus Christ. These four truths will keep you going in any wilderness. They will also enable you to be at peace and thereby good shall come unto you. They have certainly had that effect on me.

1. *He cares and He carries.*
2. *He promises and He performs.*
3. *He acts and He accomplishes.*
4. *He forgives and He forgets.*

All of those principles are found in John 6. And the centerpiece verse of John 6 in my opinion is verse 35: "Jesus said to them, 'I am the bread of life; he who comes to Me will not hunger, and he who believes in Me will never thirst.'"

In other words, Jesus is the only manna you need in any and every level of your life. That means you can depend on Him in any crisis or emergency in every aspect of your life. Nothing is too small or insignificant for Him to take notice and be available to you. If it concerns you, it concerns Him. His eye is always upon you, and He has written your name in the palm of His hand (Isa. 49:16).

Philip Ryken wrote,

Manna had the educational purpose of teaching them to depend of God for all their needs. Later Moses explained that although manna was a physical miracle, its purpose was to teach the spiritual lesson that God is the source of all our life. The prophet said, He humbled you, causing you to hunger and then feeding you with manna, which neither you nor your fathers had known, to teach you that man does not live on bread alone but on every word that comes from the mouth of God (Deut. 8:3).[1]

In John 6:48–50, Jesus declared again that He is the Bread of Life. He did not repeat something to fill in space. He did it for emphasis, and He did it to make a point. He wants us to understand that He is not only the Creator of life but the Sustainer of life. He is the Bread of Life—all of your life. He wants us to get this.

Here's the passage in fuller form:

I am the bread of life. Your fathers ate the manna in the wilderness, and they died. This is the bread that comes down from heaven, so that one may eat of it and not die. I am the living bread that came down from heaven. If anyone eats of this bread, he will live forever. And the bread that I will give for the life of the world is my flesh. (John 6:48–51 ESV)

Ryken observed the greater point:

Jesus knew that our deepest needs were not physical, but spiritual. . . . By feeding them bread He had demonstrated that he was the new and greater Moses. But the physical bread was not important. What was important was Jesus himself, who is the source of all spiritual life. . . . Jesus could do much more than multiply the bread. He was talking about himself, obviously. He was the bread, the spiritual bread from Heaven that gives life to the world.[2]

Jesus' words in those verses are what make it possible for our sins to be forgiven and for us to know that we have eternal life. Sometimes we are so stressed by our immediate difficult circumstances in the wilderness that we forget our time on this earth is brief. I am sure you have done this, and so have I. We get so hyper-focused on our immediate needs, emergencies, and exigencies that we completely lose sight of the big picture, which is that when we believe the good news of the gospel that Jesus came and died for us and gave His body and blood for the forgiveness of our sins, we are at that moment given eternal life. If He has given you eternal life and you are in a crisis that requires an immediate well-timed help, you can count on Him to give it to you. If He has promised to take care of you for eternity, why would He not take care of your immediate need? Why would He not give you the manna you need to sustain your life right now?

Don't try to reason how He will send the manna. That's a sheer waste of energy. You never can predict what He will do or how He will do it. Just tell Him about it and get yourself busy doing the next legitimate thing that needs your attention and focus. Get to work and don't try to figure out how

He will take care of you. His way and methods of sending manna are infinite and beyond imagination.

Guy and Margaret Laird experienced this firsthand many years ago when they lived in one of the most remote wildernesses of Africa.

Guy and Margaret were in trouble. The year was 1931, and they were serving as missionaries in a very remote area of what is now known as the Central African Republic. They had just returned to Africa from the United States for their second term. Their first term had ended tragically when their infant daughter had become very ill and died. They were convinced the problem was in her digestive system. While in America, Margaret consulted doctors who recommended that she take an ample supply of oatmeal and prunes in case she were to become pregnant again. When she did become pregnant, many friends encouraged Guy and Margaret not to return. What if their baby got sick out in the wilderness at Ippi? But they determined that the Lord wanted them to go, and so they did, with an ample supply of oatmeal and prunes just in case their baby became ill.

Shortly after they returned to Africa, the child of one of the other missionaries began to develop the same symptoms that had taken the life of the Lairds' infant daughter. Margaret told the woman about the advice of the American doctors and gave her the supply of oatmeal and prunes. The combination of oatmeal and prune juice over a matter of months completely cured the little girl's sickness. Everyone was thrilled.

Margaret gave birth to a little boy, and before too many months went by, her baby began to experience the dreaded symptoms. Guy and Margaret didn't want to panic, but their supply of oatmeal and prunes was gone. One afternoon the woman whose child they had helped dropped by unexpectedly. She was on her way with her family to Bambari, a town about seventy miles away. She offered to shop for Margaret, but when she saw that Margaret's list included oatmeal and prunes, she said, "That's silly, isn't it?"

Margaret was somewhat taken aback.

The woman continued, "You knew you were going to have a baby. You should have ordered those things from America. You know good and well I'll never find those things in Bambari."

Margaret was so upset by the insensitivity of this woman that she couldn't speak, but the woman was right about one thing: oatmeal and prunes were not to be found in the middle of Africa in 1931. Margaret went to the bedroom to pour out her heart to the Lord, begging Him to provide what they needed to heal their son. To paraphrase her words, she was saying:

Lord, You know all about it. If it's presumptuous, then show me and forgive me. But You are able to provide for my children in the heart of Africa, and You know that I had no money to order these things. You know I have never asked anybody to send me anything. If You are able to provide, You provide the things my children need.

Margaret said, "I was still on my knees when my husband called me. I didn't pay attention at first. He called again. I got up and went out."

Guy introduced her to two men from a Portuguese mining camp from far to the north. They had driven the long distance to talk with Guy. A young Belgium miner had recently died of sunstroke, and his very last request was that he might be buried at Ippi, as he had recently come to know Christ through reading the New Testament.

When the arrangements were made, the men got up to leave. Margaret accompanied them to the veranda.

One of them said rather nervously, "Mrs. Laird, I wonder if you would be insulted if I offered you something for the children."

"Why, not at all. I would think it was just your graciousness and God's provision."

"Well, you know we get all of our provisions from Belgium. We get two big wooden crates each month. I don't know what they think we are, but every month they send us tins of oatmeal, dried prunes, and cocoa that none of us ever use. I happen to have mine with me. Would you accept them?"[3]

Margaret was absolutely shocked. Before she had prayed her prayer, the Lord had already sent the answer. For the rest of their time in that remote little mission, she would receive every month, like clockwork, ten to twelve tins of oatmeal and dried prunes. Their little boy grew strong and healthy because the Lord sent the manna.

I say this carefully and I say it reverently—Jesus is the

Bread of Life, and in this case He was the oatmeal of life to an infant baby boy. But before we proceed, we must ask if Jesus was the Bread of Life to his infant sister who died. Why did the Lord Jesus save the little boy in such a wonderful way and not save the little girl? Such questions come out of our hearts, and we wonder if there is any answer when God seems to work so strangely. I have found Deuteronomy 29:29 to be a real help when I am bewildered by the workings of God: "The secret things belong to the LORD our God, but the things revealed belong to us and to our sons forever, that we may observe all the words of this law."

Don Carson's insights on the passage are extremely valuable to the confused believer:

> We must frankly admit that some things are hidden from our eyes. We really do not understand, for instance, the relationships between time and eternity, nor do we have much of an idea how the God who inhabits eternity discloses himself to us in our finite, space/time history. It is revealed that he does; we have various words to describe certain elements of this disclosure (e.g., Incarnation, accommodation). But we do not know how. We do not know how God can be both personal and sovereign/transcendent; we do not know how the one God can be triune.
>
> Yet in none of these cases is this a subtle appeal to ignorance, or an irresponsible hiding behind the irrational or the mystical. When we admit—indeed, insist—that

there are mysteries about these matters, we do not admit they are nonsensical or self-contradictory. Rather, we are saying that we do not know enough, and we admit our ignorance. What God has not disclosed of himself we cannot know. The secret things belong to God.

Indeed, because of the contrast in the text, the implication is that it would be presumptuous to claim we do know, or even to spend too much time trying to find out—lest we should be presuming on God's exclusive terrain. Some things may be temporarily hidden to induce us to search: Proverbs 25:2 tells us it is the glory of God to conceal a matter, and the glory of kings to search a matter out, to get to the bottom of things. But that is not a universal rule: the very first sin involved trying to know some hidden things and thus be like God. In such cases, the path of wisdom is reverent worship of him who knows all things, and careful adherence to what he has graciously disclosed.[4]

After the death of King David's child, the Lord disclosed to David's heart that he would one day join his infant son in heaven (2 Sam. 12:23). In the same way, even in the grief and loss of their daughter, the Lairds had a firm hope that they would be with their daughter forever because Jesus, the Bread of Life, conquered sin and death in His death, burial, and resurrection (1 Cor. 15:3–8).

That is a wonderful disclosure—but the great mystery is why the Lord took their daughter in infancy and allowed the son to be rescued. Psalm 139:16 declares that God determines the life span of every human being before they are born. Why do some live long lives and others do not? That is the mystery and the secret of the Lord that will only be revealed to us one day in heaven. Until then, we must bow and worship before the Lord and His wisdom and goodness.

The Lairds' little girl was taken "early" to heaven, and her brother was rescued as an infant. But for both sister and brother, their eternal life was secured for them by the Lord Jesus Christ, who is the Bread of Life, not only for this world, but for the world to come.

That same Lord is the one who miraculously sustained the Israelites in the desert and then miraculously fed twenty thousand on a hillside overlooking the Sea of Galilee. Jesus is God (John 1:1). He was the provider in Exodus 16, and He was the provider fourteen hundred years later in John 6. And He is present with us today. Jesus was and is the manna. He is the same yesterday, today, and forever.

John 6 begins with the only miracle Jesus did that is recorded in all four gospels. Some miracles are found in one gospel, others can be found in two or three, but only the feeding of the twenty thousand is found in Matthew, Mark, Luke, *and* John. Perhaps you are not familiar with the feeding of the twenty thousand. It is usually referred to as the feeding of the five thousand, but as John 6:10 makes clear, there were five thousand *men*. When you add in the women and children, twenty thousand is a conservative estimate of how many the Lord Jesus actually fed with five barley loaves and two fish.

John recorded this astonishing historical event:

After this Jesus went away to the other side of the Sea of Galilee, which is the Sea of Tiberias. And a large crowd was following him, because they saw the signs that he was doing on the sick. Jesus went up on the mountain, and there he sat down with his disciples. Now the Passover, the feast of the Jews, was at hand. Lifting up his eyes, then, and seeing that a large crowd was coming toward him, Jesus said to Philip, "Where are we to buy bread, so that these people may eat?" He said this to test him, for he himself knew what he would do. Philip answered him, "Two hundred denarii worth of bread would not be enough for each of them to get a little." One of his disciples, Andrew, Simon Peter's brother, said to him, "There is a boy here who has five barley loaves and two fish, but what are they for so many?" Jesus said, "Have the people sit down." Now there was much grass in the place. So the men sat down, about five thousand in number. Jesus then took the loaves, and when he had given thanks, he distrib-uted them to those who were seated. So also the fish, as much as they wanted. And when they had eaten their fill, he told his disciples, "Gather up the leftover fragments, that nothing may be lost." So they gathered them up and filled twelve baskets with fragments from the five barley loaves left by those who had eaten. When the people saw the sign that he had done, they said, "This is indeed the Prophet who is to come into the world!" (6:1–14 ESV)

HE CARES AND HE CARRIES

Verse 5 says, "Lifting up his eyes, then, and seeing that a large crowd was coming toward him, Jesus said to Philip, 'Where are we to buy bread, so that these people may eat?'" (ESV).

From that one verse we learn the following truth about the Lord Jesus, who is the Bread of your life and my life: He cares and He carries.

Think it through with me.

He saw the large crowd flocking to get near Him and His first thought was about their welfare. He wasn't taken with the fact that some twenty thousand people were coming to hear Him preach. His concern was not about Himself or His work or His success—it was about them.

He saw the huge crowd and his first thought was that they would need to be fed. Even though they were on the hills just above the Sea of Galilee, these people were in a type of wilderness because there were no supply lines to feed that many people.

I've had the privilege of visiting those hills where this took place, and even today there are not enough stores or fish markets around that could supply food for twenty thousand people. Two thousand years ago it would have been virtually impossible to have fed them. Many people had dropped everything and traveled for miles to see and hear Jesus. In their excitement they didn't even pack a lunch. They just took off, hoping to get a hillside seat close enough where they could actually hear Him. Food was the last thing on their minds.

Jesus knew all of this, and His interaction with Philip was one of practical necessity. These people were going to need to eat. If they didn't eat, they would lose energy, lose concentration, and quickly become fatigued.

So the Lord Jesus had everyone sit down in orderly fashion. And then He began to do for them what they couldn't do for themselves. He saved them in their crisis. He actually knew how He was to going save them before they were hungry.

And He did it because He cares.

And not only does He care, but He carries. He demonstrated His care by carrying them right through the crisis. In His hands, the five loaves and the two fish miraculously expanded into more than enough to feed all the people—with twelve baskets left over.

In Deuteronomy 1:30–31, Moses was speaking to the men of Israel who would soon go into the promised land after forty years of waiting and wandering in the wilderness. He reminded them that their fathers did not trust the Lord in spite of His care and carrying, and he did not want them to make the same mistake.

The LORD your God who goes before you will himself fight for you, just as he did for you in Egypt before your eyes, and in the wilderness, where you have seen how the LORD your God carried you, as a man carries his son, all the way that you went until you came to this place. (ESV)

He carried them because as their Father He cared for them.

Have you ever carried your little boy or girl when they were tired or fearful? You did so because you deeply cared about them. When you are in the wilderness and dealing with the adversity, there will be times you get fatigued and overwhelmed. You will run out of gas and run out of resources and all of your supply lines will be cut off. In those times, He will pick you up and carry you through stretches where you don't have the strength to make it on your own.

Don't forget in your immediate circumstances today that He cares and He carries.

Are you worried about your future?

Are you worried about losing your job or your health care?

Are you worried about getting older and how you will make it financially? What if your retirement money runs out? Or what if you have no retirement money put away? Or maybe you had retirement money put away but you lost it when the stock market crashed? How in the world are you going to make it as you get older?

Here is your answer. Jesus is the Bread of Life. Jesus is the manna. And He cares and He carries.

> Listen to me, O house of Jacob,
> And all the remnant of the house of Israel,
> You who have been borne by Me from birth
> And have been carried from the womb;
> Even to your old age I will be the same,

And even to your graying years I will bear you!
I have done it, and I will carry you;
And I will bear you and I will deliver you. (Isa. 46:3–4)

HE PROMISES AND HE PERFORMS

He has never failed on a promise. You can hold up the promises of God before Him. You're worried about your financial future, or maybe your finances day to day to day. Perhaps you are worried about a bill that is due tomorrow. Hold up Isaiah 46:3 to Him. "Hold up His Word before Him" because He cannot deny His Word. He cannot deny Himself. Jeremiah 1:12 tells us He is watching over His Word to perform it. He *will* come through. He may not come through on your time schedule, but He *will* come through.

John Flavel helps us accept the timing of God when he wrote, "Promises, like a pregnant woman, must accomplish their appointed months, and when they have so done, Providence will midwife the mercies they go big with into the world, and not one of them shall miscarry."[5]

You see, He promises and He performs. He cannot lie. It's not that He doesn't lie—He cannot lie. Titus 1:2 says, "God, who cannot lie." It's *impossible* for Him to do anything other than tell the truth. Hebrews 6:18 assures us, "It is impossible for God to lie."

So hold up the promise and wait for His timing. Psalm 84:11 declares, "No good thing does He withhold from those who walk uprightly." You may be thinking that God has withheld something from you that is good. If that is the case, hear the words of the wise pastor of the seventeenth century, Obadiah Sedgwick: "No good man ever lacked anything that was good for him. I may lack a thing which is good, but not that which is good for me. . . . Many things may be good for some people that are not always good for every man."[6] Psalm 31:19 states, "How great is Your goodness, which You have stored up for those who fear you."

God may have something in mind for you that is good, but it is not best for you right now. Can you trust Him to bring His good thing to you at the right time? If it is good for you, He has stored it away and reserved it with your name on it—and He will deliver it to you at precisely the right moment.

It is important that we carefully examine God's promises in Isaiah 46:3. We are living in troubling times that deeply distress our hearts. The foundations are being destroyed in every area of life. In times like these, as the old song used to say, we need an anchor. In times like these, we need a Savior.

Isaiah 46:3 is a gold-plated promise in the midst of the upside-down times we are living in. Society takes what is good and calls it bad. People take what is bad and call it good. It's completely irrational on every level of life. You used to be able to plan and make a financial plan. But everything is unstable right now. You know, you put some money away and save. What kind of interest are you drawing on that? Interest? You're the only one who's interested.

Remember, though, Jesus is Lord of everything, including economics. As Abraham Kuyper said, "There is not a square inch in the whole domain of our human existence over which Christ, who is Sovereign over all, does not cry, 'Mine!'"[7]

Jesus is absolutely sovereign. He is in complete control of all things.

> For by Him all things were created, both in the heavens and on earth, visible and invisible, whether thrones or dominions or rulers or authorities—all things have been created through Him and for Him. He is before all things, and in Him all things hold together. (Col. 1:16–17)

We often forget that He is the glue that holds the whole world together. And He holds your life together too. Things may look like they are out of control, but the fact is that all things are under control—His control. When we start looking around at the state of our nation and the world, we can get a little panicked sometimes. But all is not lost because He cares and He carries. He's the Bread of Life, and He will provide what you need when you need it.

My grandfather, Jubal Spurgeon Farrar, was a pastor for forty years. After he retired in his early sixties, he and my grandmother purchased a small four-unit apartment. They lived in one unit and rented the other three. As I recall, those apartments were occupied by missionaries who were either retired or getting ready to go back to the field. At some point, my grandfather became concerned about my grandmother's health. The denomination did not provide health care for retired pastors, so he took a job as a custodian for four hours in the evenings at the local elementary school to get health insurance. Then my grandfather suddenly became very ill. He was diagnosed with aggressive cancer. He was in the hospital for weeks upon weeks, and the bills were enormous. He died several months later, and the medical bills were paid by the insurance. That was manna—a well-timed help. For the longest time, my grandparents did not have health insurance. They couldn't afford it. But when they needed it, it was there.

The Lord knows more about health care than you or the government.

And He actually cares about you—and not only does He care; He will carry. He will make a way.

On the one-year anniversary of my grandfather's death, my grandmother went to be with the Lord. They had been married for over forty years. They are both now in the presence of the Lord. The Lord who through forty years of marriage, five kids, many pastorates, small salaries, and one Great Depression demonstrated that He cared and that He could carry them through any wilderness. And what He promised He did indeed perform.

Look again at the promise of Isaiah 46:3: "Listen to Me, O house of Jacob, and all the remnant of the house of Israel, you who have been borne by Me from birth."

He gave you life; He sustains your life. Don't ever forget

that. He will keep you alive until you are promoted to eternity. He has given you physical life, and He has given you eternal life.

"Yeah, that's true. But I'm really worried. Things are just crazy." So how do you fight off worry and anxiety? You have to reason your way out of worry. You have to go back to your Creator God and the promises He has made. As you look back over your life, you may remember a time when you should have died but you didn't. Perhaps you narrowly escaped death in a car crash or took a bullet in combat that lodged just a couple of centimeters from a major artery. Why didn't you die? It wasn't your appointed time (Heb. 9:27), and He carried you through the crisis. "God is to us a God of deliverances; and to GOD the Lord belong escapes from death" (Ps. 68:20).

Nothing in your life is outside of His care. Do you believe that? Proverbs 21:1 states that "the king's heart is like channels of water in the hand of the LORD; He turns it wherever He wishes."

God rules kings and rulers like you control kings and bishops on a chess board. No human heart can thwart the plan of God for your life. God is *most high*. Rulers are in their high positions because He has put them there to accomplish His purposes for a season. Read Isaiah 40—He raises up kings and He sets them down.

Your life is in God's hand. He has numbered your days, and no human can alter His plan for you. Job 14:1 and 5 state the facts: "Man, who is born of woman, is short-lived and full of turmoil. . . . Since his days are determined, the number of his months is with You; and his limits You have set so that he cannot pass."

He will be there for you in your youth and until you have finished your appointed days. No one can stay His hand or His purpose for you. He will care and He will carry you.

The economy, the administration, the rebellious child. Whatever it is that has you discouraged, He will be the same and He will be faithful. Go get some sleep if you've been worried sick about your life. This gold-plated, ironclad promise is designed to bring peace to your heart and calm your inner spirit.

You ask: "Well, how is it going to work out?" You don't need to know that. Why do *you* care? We want to know how He is going to fix things for us, but that is not our concern. Don't stay up all night trying to figure it out. Just go get some sleep. Go eat a cheeseburger. Chill out, man.

HE ACTS AND HE ACCOMPLISHES

In all areas of your life and in all your existence on the earth, God will act on your behalf, and He will accomplish what needs to be done in your life. David declared in Psalm 57:2–3, "I will cry to God Most High, to God who accomplishes all things for me. He will send from heaven and save me." Compare that with Psalm 138:8, where David stated, "The LORD will accomplish what concerns me."

He doesn't accomplish *some* things that concern you—He accomplishes *all* things that comprise His good plan for you.

Now, if you're a Christian and you're disobedient, He's going to act and accomplish some discipline to teach you. Check out Hebrews 12:5—11:

> "My son, do not regard lightly the discipline of the Lord,
> nor be weary when reproved by him.
> For the Lord disciplines the one he loves,
> and chastises every son whom he receives."

It is for discipline that you have to endure. God is treating you as sons. For what son is there whom his father does not discipline? If you are left without discipline, in which all have participated, then you are illegitimate children and not sons. Besides this, we have had earthly fathers who disciplined us and we respected them. Shall we not much more be subject to the Father of spirits and live? For they disciplined us for a short time as it seemed best to them, but he disciplines us for our good, that we may share his holiness. For the moment all discipline seems painful rather than pleasant, but later it yields the peaceful fruit of righteousness to those who have been trained by it. (ESV)

You're His child. He doesn't say, "Oh, Steve sinned again. I'm going to take him over to the orphanage and drop him off." I'm in the family. And if you have trusted Christ as your Savior, so are you. You might say, "Yeah, but I really struggle with sin, Steve." Oh, then you're reading Romans 7. Get out of Romans 7 and turn to Romans 8:1: "There is therefore now no condemnation for those who are in Christ Jesus" (ESV). There's no condemnation if you're in Christ.

"Yeah, but I really messed up." Well, then read the end of Romans 8, because nothing can separate you from the love of God. Oh, and don't miss the middle, because the whole reason nothing can separate you and there's no condemnation is that you've been judicially and legally adopted by God, and you're in the family. He acts and He accomplishes forgiveness.

But there is actually more to it than forgiveness. You might wonder, *What benefit could be added to the amazing fact that my sins are forgiven because the Lord Jesus died and paid my debt?* The amazing truth is that He not only forgives, but He forgets.

HE FORGIVES AND HE FORGETS

When the Lord forgives our sins, He actually forgets them. Hebrews 10:17–18 says, "'AND THEIR SINS AND LAWLESS DEEDS I WILL REMEMBER NO MORE.' Now where there is forgiveness of these things, there is no longer any offering for sin."

We are never to forget that He forgives and He forgets our sins.

That is why we take communion. The Lord Jesus wants us to *remember* what He did for us when He gave us His body and spilled His blood on the cross for our sins. We are to *remember* His sacrifice for our sins—all of them.

> For I received from the Lord what I also delivered to you, that the Lord Jesus on the night when he was betrayed took bread, and when he had given thanks, he broke it, and said, "This is my body which is for you. Do this in remembrance of me." In the same way also he took the cup, after supper, saying, "This cup is the new covenant in my blood. Do this, as often as you drink it, in remembrance of me." For as often as you eat this bread and drink the cup, you proclaim the Lord's death until he comes. (1 Cor. 11:23–26 ESV)

Make sure when you take communion you remember that He forgives and He forgets.

Satan wants us to remember our past sins and failures. Jesus wants us to remember Him. He wants us to remember that He is the Living Bread that has saved us from our sin forever. That's what He was saying to His disciples on the night He was betrayed by Judas.

> I am the bread of life. Your fathers ate the manna in the wilderness, and they died. This is the bread that comes down from heaven, so that one may eat of it and not die. I am the living bread that came down from heaven. If

anyone eats of this bread, he will live forever. And the bread that I will give for the life of the world is my flesh. (John 6:48–51 ESV)

Eating the bread and drinking the cup are all about remembering Him. And if you remember that He saved you forever, it makes sense that He will save you again and again as you walk through life. Romans 8:32 underscores His amazing grace: "He who did not spare his own Son but gave him up for us all, how will he not also with him graciously give us all things?" (ESV).

And one of the things He gives is His peace.

Jesus, who is the living Son of God, did this for you. Job 22:21 says, "Acquaint now thyself with him, and be at peace: thereby good shall come unto thee" (KJV).

Enjoy the peace.

It's manna from the Bread of Life.

3

STEALTH MANNA,
STEALTH PROVIDENCE

"Power belongs to God;
And lovingkindness is Yours, O Lord."

—PSALM 62:11-12

Do you remember the first time you saw a stealth fighter jet? It looked like no other jet or military aircraft you had ever seen before. And then came the stealth bomber. When those first pictures of the stealth fighter jets and bombers were leaked, I remember taking a look and thinking to myself, *What is this? I've never seen anything like this before in my entire life.*[1]

That's exactly what the Israelites thought when God

first sent the manna. The people took one look at what was on the ground and asked Moses, "What is it?" to which he replied, "It is the bread which the LORD has given you to eat" (Ex. 16:15). In other words, "It is God's provision for your need." But God's provision was not only for their food and water. When Jesus said, "I am the bread of life," He meant that He provides for *all* of life. In other words, the deeper answer to their question would have been: "It is providence."

The word *providence* is not a part of our vocabulary today. But I predict that once you come to understand it, you will find yourself using it on a daily basis. Though often hidden from the naked eye, providence is all around us. And we cannot live without it.

What is providence? Simply put, *providence* means "gracious provision." The Westminster Confession—a 1646 document crafted by a group of pastors seeking to put the Bible's teachings in a language even their children could understand— explains providence this way: "God's works of providence are his most holy, wise, and powerful works, preserving and governing all of his creatures and all of their actions."[2]

Providence is God's *detailed, purposeful, massive, daily,* and *continual* provision for His people. It is a mind-blowing concept flowing out of God's unfathomable nature: His holiness, His all-knowing wisdom, His sovereignty and omnipotence, His unchanging nature, His infinite and unconditional love, and His grace and mercy to all, especially His children. The depths of God's providence are inexhaustible and can be found on every page of Scripture.

I have a friend whose life was changed by one seemingly random event. My friend had a problem, and it was his average grades in college. When he hit thirty, he realized he wanted to make a major career shift. It would require getting into graduate school, but he knew his grades from college would make that next to impossible. He applied to nineteen different programs. As he was preparing his last application, his wife asked him about a graduate school that had recently come to his attention. He wasn't going to apply, but at her encouragement he completed one last application for that program. That gave him an even twenty. The next week he found out that he might have left one document unsigned in the twentieth application.

At his lunch hour the next day he called the dean's office to check with the dean's assistant to make sure the application was complete. The phone rang and rang, and he was about to hang up when a male voice said, "Hello." It was the dean. He was walking by the ringing phone and picked it up on a whim. That impulse turned into a forty-five-minute conversation. My friend was able to explain his situation in detail to the dean. Out of twenty applications sent, my friend got exactly one acceptance letter. But he only needed one. And he spent the next three years studying under the dean who took his call. That conversation changed the whole course of his life.

My friend was afraid that his immaturity in college was going to put him in danger of losing the career he really felt called to pursue. But stealth providence stepped in and provided manna through a phone call with the dean of a school he had not even originally applied to.

The phone call was manna, but so was his wife's suggestion at the last minute to apply. At the time, his wife's suggestion to call didn't look like manna. That's because it was stealth manna. And stealth manna is a stealth providence. It goes right under our radar, and it isn't until later that we see it as the provision of God.

John Flavel, the great preacher in England during the 1600s, was often in danger of imprisonment and death. He, along with 2,500 other Puritan preachers, was excommunicated from the state church during the Great Ejection of 1662. These men refused to go along with the unbiblical teachings held by the state church of their day. As a result, they lost their livelihoods and their freedoms, and were continually persecuted. Of course their families suffered along with them.

In September 1684, Flavel was meeting with a group of friends for prayer when soldiers broke in. He managed to escape, but his dear friend William Jenkyn was arrested and thrown in prison, where he died one year later. Such was the lot of many of those who continued to hold to the Bible in those days.

Though he was never imprisoned or killed, Flavel experienced great hardship throughout his life. The powerful men of his day hated him so much that following his death—which was honored by many Christians throughout England—the government removed his epitaph from his tomb. If anyone could speak from experience on the providence of God, this man could. In his majestic book *The Mystery of Providence,* Flavel began:

> The greatness of God is a glorious and unsearchable mystery. "For the Lord most high is terrible; he is a great king over all the earth" (Ps. 47:2). The condescension of the most high God to men is also a profound mystery. "Though the Lord be high, yet hath he respect unto the lowly" (Ps. 138:6). But when both these meet together, as they do in this Scripture, they make up a matchless mystery. Here we find the most high God performing all things for a poor distressed creature.
>
> It is a great support and solace of the saints in all the distresses that befall them here, that there is a wise Spirit sitting in all the wheels of motion, and governing the most eccentric creatures and their most pernicious designs. . . . And indeed, it were not worthwhile to live in a world devoid of God and Providence.[3]

Flavel was right. Life is not worth living in a world without God and providence.

When you are in the wilderness and all of your supply lines are cut off, what in the world can you do to fight off fear, anxiety, and worry? The cure is thinking, pondering, and chewing deeply on the truths of providence. It is the best solution in the world for fighting fear and worry. It is the key to quieting your heart and experiencing His peace in the dark places of life. And when your eyes begin to see the truth of providence, you begin to realize that it's virtually on every page of the Bible.

In this chapter we are going to look at manna in light of God's great providence. For behind every provision of manna is the stealth hand of providence. If the children of Israel had had eyes to see, they would have realized just how all-encompassing God's provision was for them in the wilderness.

For many Christians, providence has been a stealth doctrine they have not been taught or made aware of. That's why I call it stealth providence. It has flown under the radar of so many Christians. But when you get it on your radar, you understand it is a continuous gift that flows from the hand of the Lord Jesus.

He is the Bread of Life, and He upholds all things by the word of His power (Heb. 1:3). Providence is a well-timed help. Or, to put it another way, it is manna. It always shows up just in the nick of time.

IT WAS A DETAILED PROVISION

God provided for every detail of the Israelites' needs. And there were so many details! Some were huge and some were small. He provided deliverance at the Red Sea. He provided bread and water. He provided materials for their livelihood through the plundering of the Egyptians—so much material that they were able to build a tabernacle containing bronze and gold. He provided a cloud by day and a pillar of fire by night, thus leading them as they wandered without maps or compass. He prevented their clothes and sandals from wearing out as they wandered for forty years (Deut. 29:5). Each one of these provisions was a supernatural miracle.

One easily overlooked detail of God's provision for them was the maturing, humble leadership of Moses. While the people complained constantly to and about Moses, they could not have survived without him. Moses' leadership was a gift of providence.

God's people have always needed mature leaders—or shepherds, if you will—to walk by faith before them, watch over them, teach them, and lead them through crises—with genuine humility and absolute integrity. That's what makes a great leader.

Great leaders are especially needed in times of crisis. The children of Israel were no exception, so God gave them a leader. But Moses was not some young buck attempting to step into big shoes. No, God took eighty years to prepare Moses to be the leader of His people.

Moses' story of preparation is so remarkable it is worth the telling. He was born at a dangerous time, raised in a different family, and prepared in a dramatic way.

Four hundred years before his birth, the sons of Jacob had fled to Egypt during a region-wide famine. Because their brother, Joseph, was co-regent with Pharaoh, he said to them, "Bring Dad and your families; come live here, and you will be provided for." So Pharaoh built a nice subdivision for them called Goshen. Over the next four centuries, "the sons of Israel were fruitful and increased greatly, and multiplied, and became exceedingly mighty" (Ex. 1:7). In other words, they had large families and did quite well for themselves.

Then a king arose "who did not know Joseph" (v. 8). He must have had a football coach teaching him Egyptian history, because he didn't know his history. All he knew was that these sons of Israel had a birthrate that far exceeded the Egyptians. And when he did the math (he had a great math teacher), it was clear that they would soon outnumber his people. His solution was to enslave the Israelites before they enslaved him. So he appointed harsh taskmasters and turned the Israelites into slaves, imposing upon them the most grueling of labor. God had foretold this to Abraham when He said, "Know for certain that your descendants will be strangers in a land that is not theirs, where they will be enslaved and oppressed four hundred years" (Gen. 15:13).

But despite the pharaoh's best efforts, the Hebrews continued to grow in numbers. A new king feared the situation was out of control, so he issued an edict ordering that every Israelite baby boy was to be thrown into the Nile River and drowned.

Sometimes couples look around and say, "This is no time to have kids." But this *really* was no time to have kids, especially a boy. Yet Moses' parents did not let the situation keep them from the blessing of having children. So Moses was born at the worst possible time a young male could be born, until the birth of Jesus under the rule of King Herod. His mother built for him a little wicker basket covered with tar and pitch, and placed him in the reeds of the Nile for safety.

Providential Protection

What followed was God's providential protection of Moses. Pharaoh's daughter came nearby and found him. Rather than kill him, she decided to adopt him. His sister was nearby and offered to get a Hebrew wet nurse for him. And that is how his mother was able to enter the palace to nurse him, nurture him, and teach him the ways of the Lord. Providence not only saved Moses but enabled his mother to be his nanny while growing up in the "camp of the enemy," the household of Pharaoh.

What followed was God's providential upbringing of Moses. With his mother nearby, Moses was treated like a son to the king and received the best of everything. "Moses was educated in all the learning of the Egyptians, and he was a man of power in words and deeds" (Acts 7:22).

Gradually the realization of his calling came upon him. He awakened to the needs of his people and his own unique position in the land. Why was he of all people in such a place? Why had he been raised in the palace of the pharaoh while his people remained in slavery? Why had he been trained by the best military leaders while his people could not even begin to fight or defend themselves? Why was he the exception? He realized God had put him in this position for a purpose. He felt the call to step up and deliver his people.

With each passing year, the call grew heavier upon him. As he approached the age of forty, he expressed his vision to his people and even killed an Egyptian taskmaster while defending one of his Israelite brothers. But his own people rejected him, and Moses became a wanted man in the land. Fleeing into the wilderness, he saw his dream die and believed his life was over. He thought he had been called to deliver his people, and he was right. But he was forty years off.

What followed next was God's providential preparation of Moses to lead His people out of Egypt. From every viewpoint, Moses was a man who had tried to pull off a great plan and failed. He must have viewed himself as a great disappointment. But in the providence of God, He uses our failures as easily as our accomplishments. He seamlessly weaves our failures, our regrets, and our setbacks into the tapestry of purpose that He has set for our future. When we think we are finished, God continues to work His providential plan. It was Thomas Watson who observed that "God enriches by impoverishing. . . . God works strangely. He brings order out of confusion, harmony out of discord. . . . God often helps when there is least hope, and saves his people in that way which they think will destroy."[4]

When Moses fled to the wilderness, he was confused, defeated, out of hope, and no doubt wondering if the pursuit of Pharaoh would end his life. He had no idea that God was using his failure to get him out of Egypt so that he could be prepared in the sands of the wilderness. The Lord wasn't finished with Moses when he failed, and He isn't finished when you fail. It's simply another tool in His workshop that He uses to accomplish His purpose in our lives and in His grand plan.

And for Moses, the Lord had determined a most unlikely preparation. God used the wilderness to build Moses into the man who could handle the taxing but important job that lay ahead. Moses did not know it, but he was in the Master's workshop.

There was nothing glorious or self-inflating in the wilderness, only isolation, depravation, and obscurity. This man who had worn only the finest clothes and eaten the finest foods was now wearing shepherd's clothing, herding a bunch of dirty sheep, and searching day and night for water and food for himself and his sheep. Flavius Josephus, the first-century Roman Jewish historian, said that before this deflating stint in the wilderness, Moses had been "a military leader. He led an all-night march in which he took back the city of Memphis, which had been captured by the Cushites. He captured them and came back to a hero's welcome in Egypt. He was trained in all the learning of the Egyptians."[5] Moses had been the General Schwarzkopf of his day. He had held the equivalent of a PhD in the ancient Egyptian Semitic universities. He was a natural-born leader. And now he was leading a bunch of bleating sheep.

This leadership course—call it Wilderness Crisis Management 101—was not offered in Pharaoh's schools. It required the tutoring of the Lord Himself in the desolation of an arid land. Much like our Navy SEAL training of today, it was a hardcore, extreme regimen over an excruciatingly long period of time. But the Lord knew what it would take to get Moses ready.

Eventually Moses married and became the father of two sons. And over those forty years in a harsh and unforgiving wilderness, some interesting things began to take shape within Moses. He lost his cockiness and bravado, as well as his sense of self-entitlement. He learned the value of patience and endurance, the importance of taking life one day at a time, and the reward of serving. In the wilderness—except for perhaps killing a lion or two—his military training was useless. In the wilderness—except for the calling of his sheep when they wandered off—his gifts of leadership were wasted. Sheep care absolutely nothing about what you say to them unless you are calling them to eat or drink. And though God had a plan for all of Moses' training and gifts, He also had an equally purposeful plan for those long, wearisome, seemingly wasted years in the wilderness.

One day the time came for Moses to leave the wilderness. So God appeared to him in a burning bush and reissued the call Moses had felt so strongly as a younger man. This time he was needy and humbled; he no longer trusted in his own ability to persuade or lead anyone. Which was exactly where God wanted him to be. He was ready to be used.

It was providence that so painstakingly prepared the right man to lead God's people at the right time out of Egypt and through the wilderness. What an amazing providence!

God's providence is at work in all the details of your life, and He persists all through your days. He sees it all. He controls it all. He works in it all and uses it all for your good and the glory of His name.

No matter what the situation is, God is sovereign over every detail of it. "But seek first His kingdom and His righteousness, and *all these things* will be added to you," Jesus promised in Matthew 6:33 (emphasis added). What things? All the things you need. The things that you will eat and drink and wear, the things required for you to have shelter, the things required for you to take care of your family. God knows it all, and He will provide it all. He will get the manna to you at the right time. He knows every hair on your head (Luke 12:7), and He promises to provide for your needs, both great and small.

The children of Israel experienced providence in every detail of life, but it never changed the unbelief in their hearts or gave them peace of mind. Providence is supplied to quiet our hearts and give us confidence for our today and tomorrows.

Thomas Watson, who knew many sorrows and persecutions in his own life, observed:

This is not the first strait we have been in nor the first time that our hearts and hopes have been low. Surely He is the same God now as heretofore, His hand is not shortened, neither does His faithfulness fail. O recount in how great extremities former experience has taught you not to despair . . . the experiences we have had throughout our lives of the faithfulness and constancy of Providence are of excellent use to allay and quiet our hearts in any trouble that befalls us. "Hitherto hath the Lord helped us" (1 Sam. 7:12).[6]

IT WAS A PURPOSEFUL PROVISION

They did not know it, but God's provision held a greater purpose than merely meeting a need. It was for their instruction and growth. It was for the building up of their faith.

Speaking of Moses, Hebrews 11 says, "By faith he left Egypt, not fearing the wrath of the king; for he endured, as seeing Him who is unseen. . . . By faith they passed through the Red Sea as though they were passing through dry land; and the Egyptians, when they attempted it, were drowned" (vv. 27, 29).

A. W. Pink, in his book *Gleanings in Exodus*, explained:

The leading of Israel into the Wilderness of Sin [a particular region] brings out the strength of Moses' faith. Here, for the first time, the full privation of desert life stared the people fully in the face. Every step they took was now leading them farther away from the inhabited countries and conducting them deeper into the land of desolation and death. The isolation of the wilderness was complete, and the courage and faith of their leader in bringing a multitude of at least two million people into such a howling waste, demonstrates his firm confidence in the Lord God. Moses was not ignorant of the character of this desert. He had lived for forty years in its immediate vicinity.[7]

Having survived in this wilderness when he fled Egypt, Moses knew its difficulties. But let's face it; it is one thing to forage for a wife and a couple of kids. It's another thing to lead two million men, women, and children into the desert and oversee their care. Yet when God said, "Go in," Moses went.

How was he able to do this? He walked not by sight but by faith. His eyes were not on the external circumstances or the supply lines or the budget or the shortfall. His eyes were on the living God who had already done many miracles to bring about their exodus and deliverance at the Red Sea. Knowing full well what lay ahead, Moses also "knew full well that only a miracle, yea, a series of daily miracles, could meet the vast needs of such a multitude. In this his faith was superior to Abraham's," wrote Pink.[8]

In the Old and New Testaments, we read that God always had His people walking by faith. You can expect that there will be some area of your life that you cannot control, that you can't get your arms around, that you cannot fix, and that only God can accomplish. You are completely and totally dependent on Him.

When you and I find ourselves in such a place and when God provides at such a time, He is teaching us to walk by faith. Each time He provides, He is saying, "Remember this.

Know that I am God. You can trust Me." From one providence to the next, He is building our faith. He is teaching us
to walk by faith.

In his little book *Concise Theology*, J. I. Packer wrote
about God's purposeful work through providence:

> If Creation was a unique exercise of divine energy caus-
> ing the world to be, providence is a continued exercise of
> that same energy whereby the Creator, according to his
> own will, (a) keeps all creatures in being, (b) involves
> himself in all events, and (c) directs all things to their
> appointed end. This model is a purposeful personal man-
> agement with total "hands-on" control.[9]

There is a purpose behind God's providential work in
our lives. He is turning us into men of faith. It is providence
that takes us into the wilderness, it is providence that sustains us, and it is providence that brings us out. In the end, it
is providence that builds us into mature men.

If the goal is to learn how to walk by faith and not by
sight, then you can always know the hidden purpose behind
your wilderness. When God is building a man, He begins
by taking his strong will and breaking it down. He takes his
dreams and aspirations and crushes them. Then He redirects
his life and begins to rebuild him. This is how God works in
every man who will be used by Him.

Have you been called to leadership, just as Moses was?
Yes. There are people looking to you. They are looking to

you at work, and they are looking to you at home. Know this: when hardship comes, God is shaping you, building you, and equipping you to be a mature leader in every sphere of your life, especially in your home.

God's hidden hand is in every event that occurs in your life. In each one His stealth yet purposeful providence is at work.

IT WAS A MASSIVE PROVISION

When God provided manna for the people, He gave instructions for them to measure out an omer of manna per person. How many of you have a measuring cup for an omer in your kitchen? If you are like me, you don't even know if you have a spatula in your kitchen. An omer is the equivalent of six pints.

Now consider that each person was to gather six pints. For two million people, God had to send twelve million pints, or nine million pounds, or four thousand five hundred tons of manna each morning. It is hard to fathom that amount. Yet—except for the Sabbath—it was there every single day.

Manna was a massive provision.

Today that amount of manna would require ten trains, each having thirty cars, and each car carrying fifteen tons— for a *single* day's supply.

We have no coal mines in our state, but most of our electricity comes from coal. So we have trains that come regularly from Kansas, their cars filled to the brim with coal from Pennsylvania, Montana, and West Virginia. If those supply lines were ever cut off, we would be looking for grandpa's kerosene lamp. That coal keeps us going. In the same way, God's massive provision kept His people going. It was important that the children of Israel did not die out, because one day this nation would produce the Messiah and Savior of the world.

But God's massive provision is not only for His people. It is for the whole world. We tend not to think of this as we walk through our day. Yet God's stealth providence is massive in its scope. Silently but certainly our God keeps our world going. Were it not for His provision, the creatures of the earth would not have air to breathe, or water to drink, or food to eat. Gravity would not remain in force. The earth would spin into space and self-destruct. Why? Because "in Him all things hold together" (Col. 1:17).

Christ holds the cosmos in place, and every atom of every molecule continues to function at His command. The rain falls at His command, and the sun continues to shine at His command. The oceans keep their boundaries and sustain the vast creatures of the sea—at His command. Here's how David, the psalmist, perceived things: "You visit the earth and cause it to overflow; You greatly enrich it; the stream of God is full of water; You prepare grain, for this You prepare the earth" (Ps. 65:9).

He owns it all. And though we may not see or acknowledge it, we could not exist without God's stealth yet massive provision.

IT WAS A DAILY AND
CONTINUAL PROVISION

The children of Israel had only enough manna for a given day. Each night their cupboards were empty, and once again they faced potential bankruptcy and starvation.

Do you go to bed at night worried about your bank account? For some of us right now, no matter how frugal we have been, no matter how carefully we have planned, it is still tight. We understand the Hebrew man lying in his bed in the wilderness and wondering if God's provision was going to show up the next day.

Matthew Henry wrote, "'Let them learn to go to bed and sleep quietly, though they have not a bit of bread in their tent, nor in all their camp, trusting that God, with the following day, will bring them their daily bread.' It was surer and safer in God's storehouse than in their own, and would thence come to them sweeter and fresher."[10]

God brings manna to us just as He did the Israelites. If you are in a season in which you have nothing stored up, it is okay. Go to sleep. Because He gives to His beloved even in their sleep (Ps. 127).

On the other hand, if you are in a season of financial security, even then you are dependent upon God for your daily provision. No economy is guaranteed to be safe and sound. No job is totally secure. No one's health is assured. All can be lost quickly, even at a moment's notice. Each of us is dependent every day of our lives on God's gracious provision.

The apostle Paul gave young Timothy some clear direction on this point when he wrote, "Instruct those who are rich in this present world not to be conceited or to fix their hope on the uncertainty of riches, but on God, who richly supplies us with all things to enjoy" (1 Tim. 6:17).

Ultimately, our daily salvation "does not depend on the man who wills or the man who runs, but on God who has mercy" (Rom. 9:16). I like that. I need to heed and embrace that truth. So do you. That's manna.

John Flavel, who began our chapter, was a man without a means of income for most of his life. Flavel knew what it was to depend upon God for daily manna. He wrote,

> The care of Providence runs parallel with the line of life. . . . You know the promises God has made to His people: "The young lions do lack and suffer hunger, but they that seek the Lord will not want any good thing" (Ps. 34:10). And have you not also seen the constant performance of it? Can you not give the same answer, if the question were propounded to you, which the disciples did: "When I sent you without purse, and scrip, and shoes, lacked ye anything? and they said, Nothing" (Luke 22:35)? . . . His mercies "are new every morning" (Lam. 3:23).[11]

Providence is daily and continual. "Surely goodness and lovingkindness will follow me *all the days of my life*, and I will dwell in the house of the LORD forever," exclaimed David (Ps. 23:6, emphasis added).

There is yet one more aspect of providence worth considering.

IT WAS A SURPRISING PROVISION

Manna was certainly not the norm. Who could have ever thought of such a thing? But God's ways are not our ways.

Our lives take unexpected turns. And oftentimes the provision of God comes in a way that we least expect. Abraham believed God when He promised to make him the father of a nation, but he did not expect to give birth to a child when he was a hundred years old. Joseph never imagined as he prayed to the Lord in a prison cell that he would find himself one day ruling in the palace. Moses had no clue he would be leading two million people through a desert. He thought he would be taking them into the promised land, but God had other plans for Moses.

We don't know what the Lord is going to do. We don't know how He plans to do it. We just have to trust in Him and show up.

One surprising providence in my own life occurred when I was a young man. I was in seminary in Oregon, working the truck docks to get by, until the economy went south, I was laid off, and my funds began to run out. I realized I had to leave school and go back home in order to earn some money. When one of my buddies saw me packing, he said, "Hey, Steve, don't leave just yet. I think I know someone who can help you stay in school." He told me about a godly older friend who was the CEO of one of the largest companies in the state and gave generously out of his abundance.

A few days later I found myself headed down for an appointment with him. I walked into his enormous office on the top floor of an impressive high-rise in downtown Portland. He greeted me warmly.

He said, "I've been told you've been going to seminary but have been laid off from work." I explained that I was only hoping to find work in the area so I could finish seminary. He said, "I think it would be good if you could stay in school. Can you come back tomorrow at four? Let me see what I can do." I said, "Yes, sir. I appreciate that." He was very gracious and gave me a great deal of time.

The next afternoon I walked into his office, and he said, "I'm sorry I have nothing for you. Thank you for coming in." Then he rose and shook my hand. He was the total opposite of what he had been the day before. I was stunned and wondered if I had done something to offend him.

I said to him, "Sir, I appreciate your time. I just want to clarify something. I understood yesterday that you wanted me to come back in to see you today. Was that right?" He said, "Absolutely, and thank you for coming back."

His demeanor was polite but very businesslike. I was in and out of his office in less than five minutes. This was a complete switch from his warmth and supportiveness the day before. I remember walking down the steps of that massive skyscraper and thinking to myself, *That was so weird, it had to be from God.*

What happened in that office? I don't really have an explanation. He was a fine Christian man who was a serious follower of Christ. He wasn't playing games with me or giving me false hope. In hindsight, I think it was a turn of events from the Lord. The Lord simply wanted to move me out into another chapter that I knew nothing of. For that year, He did not want me to be in seminary studying books. He was going to send me to the sands of Tucson and give me some real-life training in a church. But I knew nothing about that when I walked out of the high-rise building. All I knew was that I was leaving to go home and find some work in California.

I packed up my Volkswagen and went home. When I got there, I went to the truck docks of San Jose to look for work and was told that things were pretty tight there too but maybe I could pick up a shift here and there. I had brought home all these books that were collateral reading for my seminary classes, so I did a large amount of reading between shifts. I realized I had been so focused on getting my degree and so busy making that happen that I had had little time to think and actually learn. It was a great time for me.

Four months later, I was told I would be given a full-time graveyard shift in two weeks. I would be able to earn enough money to be back in school by the next January. Excellent.

That Sunday night I went to Peninsula Bible Church

where they held a weekly service called Body Life. It was packed to the gills with college students and other young people from my generation. The meeting was free flowing, with people getting up and asking for prayer or sharing what God was doing in their lives. It seemed like every person who spoke was struggling and up against the wall. I felt compelled to share the answer to prayer the Lord had just given me that week. So I got up and said, "I just want to say thanks to the Lord, because I have been waiting for four months for a job, and just this week I found out that I am going to start a full-time job in two weeks. That means I will be able to earn enough money to go back to seminary. I just wanted to say that if you are discouraged, He answers prayer. Just hang in there."

At the end of the service, a guy in his thirties made a bee-line for me. He said, "Do I know you from somewhere?" We figured out that I had once been in Arizona with a ministry team and visited his church one Sunday. Soon we realized we had a few other connections, and then he told me he was in the Bay Area looking for someone from Body Life to co-pastor his church in Arizona.

We decided to go get coffee and ended up talking for several hours. We discovered that we were both from the same denominational background and both working through the same issues in the Bible. And because I was a few years out ahead of him in the search, he began asking me questions. We had a great connection. Before the night was over, he explained that he was taking his church on the same journey and needed help in teaching them the Bible. Then he said, "I think you are the guy to help me."

"I guarantee you I'm not your guy. I'm going to finish seminary. And I just landed a full-time job that will enable me to finish out the program." I explained to him that I needed to make money to go to seminary. And I could make some very good money working on the docks in just six months and be back in seminary for the winter semester. We talked another hour or so and I was emphatic that I was not the guy he needed.

Two days later he called from Arizona. He asked how much I would make in my job. I told him, and then he invited me to come fly down that weekend and preach for him on Sunday. I had never preached in a church on a Sunday morning before so it was a unique opportunity. I told him I would come and preach as long as he knew I wasn't a candidate. Well, you can figure out what happened.

I went down and preached, met the elders, and they offered me a pastoral internship for six months. And they said they would match the pay of the other job.

I accepted the job. During that time I was able to regularly preach and take the elders through a study of theology. I learned more about ministry there than I could have ever learned in seminary. Most surprising of all, at the end of my time the elders told me they would pay for the rest of my seminary training.

I had gone from a very tall, impressive building—where I thought God would take care of my needs—to a little congregation in Arizona—where my needs, and more, were met beyond anything I could have possibly imagined.

God sent manna. But at first I didn't want the manna. I wanted my plan and I wanted it my way. But the Lord had a stealth providence for me. When you are in a wilderness, watch God's unexpected, stealth providence at work. Then when your children are old enough, tell them your own stories of our amazing God.

They'll remember those stories years later when they visit the wilderness.

Stealth providence is His faithfulness to *all* generations.

4

HIS TIME, HIS TIMING

"When my anxious thoughts
multiply within me,
Your consolations delight my soul."

—Psalm 94:19

Anxious thoughts never run solo; anxious thoughts hunt in packs. They stalk you—relentless in their pursuit of whatever peace you may have managed to preserve—until through fear, intimidation, and ultimately one final assault, they overwhelm and surround you, each thought snarling and biting, smelling blood. Your resolve and faith weakened by the drain of worry, finally paralyzed, you succumb. Easy prey.

If you step back and objectively analyze the thoughts

you've entertained, you will discover that their combined force reduces to one central question: "What if God doesn't come through for me?"

What you need in all that anxiety is manna.

In 1995, I found myself in a place I never imagined. It was remarkable because the Lord was doing something very unique among men. I had left the pastorate to go into full-time ministry to men in 1990. That was something I never intended to do. But in the providence of God, I had written a book for men in 1990 called *Point Man*. It was all about how a man could become a spiritual leader. I knew exactly two men in the country who were in full-time men's ministry, so let's just say it wasn't a crowded field. Churches tended to focus on children's ministry, women's ministry, youth ministry, senior citizens ministry—but not men's ministry. In my opinion, men were the sleeping giants of the evangelical church. If you could get the men, you would have the wives and kids. In my mind, men were very strategic. But in most churches across the country, men were an afterthought. No one knew in 1990 that the Lord was getting ready to change that.

I came out with *Point Man* and was hoping that the phone would ring so that I could set up some men's conferences. That first year we got somewhere between three and four hundred calls from churches asking me to come and speak to their men. The churches were using *Point Man*, but they wanted a conference for their guys, and suddenly I was busier than I could imagine. At the same time, the Promise Keepers movement started filling football stadiums across the country.

I found myself speaking in front of forty to seventy thousand men in stadiums and racetracks across the country.

By 1995, I had a staff of seven and I was in desperate need of someone to oversee the ministry and free me up to study, speak, and write. I was getting spread out way too thin in trying to add the oversight of the ministry to my list. I found the management piece to be incredibly draining because I simply don't have the gifts for it. I needed a very special individual with rare leadership and administrative gifts who could take the ministry side of things off of me and enable me to focus on speaking and writing. For months and months we looked and prayed for the right person.

One night as I was getting into bed, Mary looked up from her book and said, "Steve, you just seem so frustrated."

"Well, I really am. I needed to spend the day writing and all I did was put out fires at the office. I've got to get someone to help me, and I need them right away. I've got a deadline coming up on a book, and I keep getting pulled to details at the office. I need another draft horse to pull this wagon!"

As Mary and I talked about it, she said wouldn't it be wonderful if the Lord would bring in someone with the skills I needed, whom I could trust and take this load off of me. She went into some detail, and I stopped her and said, "What you're describing is someone who could run a Fortune 500 company."

"Well, wouldn't it be great if the Lord gave you someone like that who shared your heart for men's ministry?"

"Mary, I've got seven people. The kind of man you're

describing wouldn't even consider something as small as our ministry."

And then she said, "You ought to ask Dean Gage to come on board with you."

I almost laughed out loud. Dean had become a good friend in the past year. He was the former president of Texas A&M University, and we had met at the Astrodome in Houston during a Promise Keepers event. He then invited me to do a conference for about a thousand men at his church. Dean certainly had a heart for the Lord and for equipping men for the kingdom. He was a man who had stood for Christ in the academic world. He was a great leader and a real servant. The reason that I almost laughed was that Dean was so over-qualified for our little small ministry. And I told Mary a guy like Dean would never even consider such a thing. He had been responsible for approximately twenty thousand faculty and staff at A&M.

And then she said, "Well, maybe he wouldn't, but you'll never know unless you ask him." Mary has very good instincts and a unique track record in sensing the Lord's guidance, but I thought she was way out to lunch on this one.

And then I remembered that Dean had sent me a note saying he was going to be in Dallas the next week and would like to have lunch with us if we were free. I mentioned that to Mary and she said, "Well, there you go. You can ask him next week at lunch."

"Well, let's have lunch with him for sure, but there's no way I'm going to embarrass myself by even bringing this up."

We had a great lunch and most of our conversation was about the importance of equipping men to be spiritual leaders in their homes, but I was still very reluctant to broach the subject with him. Dean and I were of one mind on the absolute importance of equipping men to first lead in their homes and then in their churches. I said, "Well, Dean, wouldn't it be something if at some point we could work together in achieving that goal?"

He looked at me, started to say something, and then dropped his eyes to the table. He didn't say anything for the longest time. I really thought I had offended him. I glanced over at Mary. We were both riveted by the moment. And then he looked at me and said, "I've been praying for eight months that you would ask me."

I was stunned. I then said, "Well, Dean, why didn't you just bring it up?" He replied, "I didn't want to do that. But I've had such a desire to work with you in the ministry. But I felt that if the Lord were in it, He would put it on your heart to approach me."

Two weeks later he was on board, and just in the nick of time. It was another mercy, it was another well-timed help, and it was another provision of manna at just the right time.

Manna was there every morning for God's people in the wilderness. Centuries later, Jeremiah the prophet proclaimed that the Lord's mercies "are new every morning; great is Your faithfulness" (Lam. 3:23).

That's *every* morning. Like clockwork. As sure as the sun rises, His mercies renew. For your family. For your marriage.

For your kids. For every level and aspect of your life. Every morning. You and I should thank God for the railroad cars of grace that we have enjoyed up until now. But we are going to go to sleep tonight and, as great as His grace was today, it has been used up. We will need a fresh boxcar tomorrow.

The children of Israel could have gone to bed at night and worried themselves sick about whether the manna would be there in the morning. But God never missed. Yet in the thick of challenging circumstances, anxiety mounts, worry takes hold, fear sets in. And what you need again is some well-timed help.

Timing is critical. Pressure puts the squeeze on time. And the closer you get to the deadline, the greater the stress and anxiety. David, under duress, confessed, "When my anxious thoughts multiply within me, Your consolations delight my soul" (Ps. 94:19). David had learned that even in times of anxiety the Lord would provide what he needed—manna in just the right time.

The Lord's provision enables you to fight off anxiety and fight off fear in the midst of looming pressure, a pressing deadline, an ominous diagnosis. In those settings the Lord sends His manna.

David called those provisions His *consolations*. Jeremiah calls them His *mercies*. What are the Lord's consolations and mercies? They are manna just in time. They come from His Word. His promises. His personal presence. His peace. Those are the Lord's consolations and mercies.

For forty years God showed up on time with the manna.

He never missed once. It was there when it was supposed to be there. It was never early and it was never late. Everything came just in time. That's how God works.

JUST-IN-TIME GOD

Steve Saint grew up on the mission field in South America. When Steve was five years old, his father, Nate, and four other missionaries, including Jim Elliot, were murdered by Huaorani Indians.

Steve eventually moved back to the States, graduated from college, and went into the home-building business. In May 1981, interest rates were at 15 percent. No one was buying homes, not even prosperous families. Steve was feeling great pressure. He and his partner had employees who needed work, but he didn't have any work for them to do. He felt bad because he had taken some months off to go to Ecuador to help construct a hydroelectric dam in the Andes that would supply power for the World Radio Missionary Fellowship. It was a bad time to leave, but his partner told him to go if he felt the Lord was calling him and assured Steve the Lord would take care of the business. So Steve went, and the project was completed in a remarkable way.

But when he returned, he felt guilty for having left at such a bad time. Winter was about to hit Minnesota, and he needed to line up projects for the spring. On one particular morning, Steve was asking the Lord to do the impossible. He was desperate for some business. He knew the Lord could do anything, despite the terrible economy. He asked the Lord to send him a customer that morning who was ready, willing, and able to buy. In fact, he asked the Lord to give him a signed contract on a house by noon that very day. As soon as he prayed that prayer, he regretted it—he knew he was asking for a miracle.

Later that morning he heard a car pull up in front of his office, and his hopes soared. But then he saw the old car and the two women step out of it. From the way they were dressed, it was obvious they did not have much money. In fact, from their dress he guessed they were from South America, and it turned out he was right.

The two ladies were seated, and the older one spoke to the younger in Spanish. Before the younger woman could translate, Steve responded in fluent Spanish. The ladies were shocked. The older lady told Steve she wanted to get a subsidized government loan to buy a house. Steve and his partner didn't do this kind of work primarily because of the incredible red tape that the government required, and there wasn't much of a profit in small houses to begin with. His hopes for a signed contract by noon went out the window.

Due to the language barrier, he offered to call the Farmers Home Administration for the older lady. Steve made the call, and it seemed to take forever to get a human being on the other end. When the woman answered, he quickly explained the situation. He told the woman he had a migrant family who wanted to buy with a government loan. "Are they

Spanish?" the woman asked. "Is she still in your office? Does she like any of your plans? Is there any way you could come with her right now to our office?"

The agent explained to Steve that they were about to lose their government funding because they had not made any loans to migrant families. None. The fact was there were hardly any Hispanic migrant families in Wilmar, Minnesota, in 1981.

Steve told the rest of the story:

> Grandma's was the first application our FmHA office had received from an honest-to-goodness minority, and they needed her more than she needed the house. They needed me because I could translate. They also needed the contract signed as soon as possible to avoid losing their funding. The only aspect of the normal modus operandi they didn't change was the truckload of forms that had to be filled out.
>
> By the time we were done the at FmHA office, I was worn out. . . . I headed back to my own office. I glanced down at my watch. Twelve o'clock—noon![1]

It was manna for Steve and his partner. It was a well-timed help from the Bread of Life. And the Lord kept the manna coming—as Steve said, "The Lord's plan was bigger than his imagination." Another FmHA buyer came and then another, and within three weeks he had sold eight houses. It was a time of unusual financial blessing in a horrible economy. And it actually made it possible for Steve to fund another mission project in Africa.

Nothing is too hard for the Lord. Steve Saint found that out firsthand.

Even if it's a request for a noon deadline, God is the originator of just-in-time inventory.

Manna is all about timing. Live long enough and you will find yourself, just like the Israelites, in great need of a well-timed help. And because He is Lord of every area of your life, He has the ability to come through for you at any level.

If manna is about timing, then you need to know what God says about time and timing in general. I find at least seven principles in Scripture that are each worth a bit of reflection.

1. God Owns Time.

God is eternal. He is preexistent, which means He lives outside of and transcends time. He is also the Creator of time. Time stands ready at God's command to submit as a servant to His will. Time does not constrain or control God. God constrains and controls time. He invented time. He's got the copyright and the patent on time. He owns it.

In the gospel of John there's an exchange between Jesus and the Pharisees that describes the Lord's transcendence and power over time.

The Pharisees notoriously despised Jesus for His continual exposure of their evil hearts. They foamed with hatred and grew more and more desperate to eliminate Him. Listen in as the drama unfolds.

> Jesus answered them, ". . . I know that you are Abraham's descendants; yet you seek to kill Me, because My word has no place in you. . . . But as it is, you are seeking to kill Me, a man who has told you the truth, which I heard from God; this Abraham did not do." (John 8:34, 37, 40)

Stung by Jesus' charge, the Pharisees then accused Him of being born illegitimately, a son of Satan—a blasphemous reconstruction of the supernatural circumstances of His conception and birth to a virgin.

Jesus didn't blink. Instead, He rebuked them sharply, replying, "You are of your father the devil, and you want to do the desires of your father. He was a murderer from the beginning. . . . Whenever he speaks a lie, he speaks from his own nature, for he is a liar, and the father of lies. But because I speak the truth, you do not believe Me" (John 8:44–45).

He was only warming to His point. He continued, "'Your father Abraham rejoiced to see My day, and he saw it and was glad.' So the Jews said to Him, 'You are not yet fifty years old, and have You seen Abraham?' Jesus said to them, 'Truly, truly, I say to you, before Abraham was born, I am'" (John 8:56–58).

Jesus declared boldly, "I am God." He is the same God who spoke to Abraham at the burning bush. Fully and completely eternal, without beginning or end. In other words, He is the almighty God who actually created time and brought it into existence.

The Pharisees understood fully what Jesus meant by that expression. That's why they took up stones to try to kill Him. Claiming deity warranted an immediate and violent death according to the Law. And Jesus had just claimed deity

Not coincidentally, however, that provocative expression came from the wilderness narrative. And it was manna for anxious times.

After God heard the cry of His people suffering under bondage to Pharaoh, He set out to recruit Moses to be their deliverer. In Exodus 3, God introduced Himself to Moses at the burning bush using the same expression Jesus used to rebuke His sneering opponents.

Moses had asked in his infamous reluctance,

> "I am going to the sons of Israel, and I will say to them, 'The God of your fathers has sent me to you.' Now they may say to me, 'What is His name?' What shall I say to them?" God said to Moses, "I AM WHO I AM"; and He said, "Thus you shall say to the sons of Israel, 'I AM has sent me to you.'" (Ex. 3:13–14)

God simply stated that He is eternal; He has no beginning and no end. He is uncreated; He remains eternally existent and self-sustaining. God has always been and He always will be. He existed before the beginning of time, because He has always been in existence. Is this blowing your mind yet?

There has never been a moment in which God was not. God is incomprehensible. He is knowable, but wholly incomprehensible.

When Jesus said, "I AM," He declared, "I am the self-existent God." That's why He could say that before Abraham existed, "I AM." Jesus created Abraham. He created the world. He is God.

John wrote, "In the beginning was the Word, and the Word was with God, and the Word was God. He was in the beginning with God. All things came into being through Him, and apart from Him nothing came into being that has come into being" (John 1:1–3).

Jesus is the eternal God who has always existed. Jesus, the Bread of Life, created time. The One who promises to provide you with well-timed help does not want you to be anxious about time. Because He's not. Time does not restrain Him or control Him. *He* restrains and controls time.

2. God Appoints the Times.

The turning of the earth and its fixed times and seasons—summer, fall, winter, spring—are all appointed by God for His eternal purposes.

As the Israelites prepared to enter the promised land, God gave to them certain sacred seasons. These were to be part of their national calendar, just as we have sacred seasons on our calendars. There were three times set aside each year in which the Israelite men were to bring their families to the tabernacle—and in later years, to the temple in Jerusalem.

Since two out of three of those festivals had to do with harvests, God intended that they should experience not only a time of celebration but also a time of corporate worship. But how did these people know when they were to meet up for these festivals? They didn't have an atomic clock or an iPad. None of that was available. Instead, they had the sun, the moon, and the stars.

At creation, God put the heavenly bodies in place to light the universe and to determine the seasons of the earth. Since creation, God's people have ordered their lives by the changing of those seasons and the movement of those celestial bodies. Just as the movement of the sun by day was their wristwatch, so the movement of these vast galaxies of the night provided an annual calendar.

High above the plains of Colorado is a place you can drive to that is part of the great Continental Divide. No billboards or streetlamps or gaudy strip-mall lights are present to veil or contaminate the night skies. In that perfect darkness, the one hundred billion stars of the Milky Way spread out before you and overwhelm you with an amazing brilliance. And it doesn't matter whether you visited there last year or fifty years ago. The drama of that celestial lightshow remains the same. That's because those billions of stars are fixed stars. And their movements are so impeccably reliable that an ancient traveler could literally gauge his calendar and find his way through the darkness by their positioning.

For forty long and arduous years in the desert, the Israelites gazed upon that wondrous display of fixed points each night. God promised that "while the earth remains, seedtime and harvest, and cold and heat, and summer and winter, and day and night shall not cease" (Gen. 8:22). The annual seasons on the earth have been fixed by God, and they will never cease.

Thirty years ago, certain scientists and media outlets were predicting global freezing. Now the big prediction is global warming. No doubt yet another prediction will be coming down the pike in the coming years. But whatever the current alarm—whether it is that the earth is going to freeze or turn into a waterless desert—God has revealed clearly that seedtime and harvest time, cold and heat, summer and winter, day and night "shall not cease." It's all in His plan.

We can trust His word on that because He ordains the time. He orders and determines time. He keeps time going.

But God appoints more than the times of our seasonal calendar. He also appoints the times of human history—the rise and fall of nations and all of those events of human history that follow, one upon the other, century after century, for His holy and gracious purpose. God has a plan for the ages.

In the Old Testament book of Daniel, God revealed to His prophet many mysterious events that would shape all times in the future. Repeatedly Daniel used the phrase "at the appointed time" this will happen, and "at the appointed time" that will happen (8:19; 11:27, 29, 35).

Without question, God has a plan for the ages, and history

is going somewhere. And it all unfolds *at the appointed time.* God is the great Appointer and Keeper of the times. This is not chaos. God is moving the world toward His great purposes, and there is a prophetic plan. It is on schedule to the nanosecond. It is more exact than an atomic clock.

And all of these things are appointed and fixed by God.

And that includes you and your existence.

3. God Changes the Times.

The older I get, the more resistant to change I become. That's certainly part of human nature. In 586 BC, a young Israelite named Daniel was taken off to Babylon, and the nation of Judah went into captivity for seventy years. Daniel was part of the royal internship program with his three friends serving under King Nebuchadnezzar. One night the king had a disturbing dream, so disturbing that he gathered his wise men and threatened them with death if they could not interpret the meaning of his nightmare.

They got concerned because there was nobody on earth who could do that. But since God controls all things and transcends time, He powerfully revealed the details of the king's dream to Daniel.

Then the mystery was revealed to Daniel in a night vision. Then Daniel blessed the God of heaven. Daniel said,

"Let the name of God be blessed forever and ever, For wisdom and power belong to Him.

It is He who changes the times and the epochs;
He removes kings and establishes kings."
(Dan. 2:19–21)

In other words, when times change, it is not simply a change created by human ideas or movements or revolutions. Ultimately God orchestrates these symphonic movements of change in the times and epochs of history. Sometimes we are excited by the times. Sometimes depression and fear flow from more difficult and uncertain times. Sometimes we look around and see things deteriorating for the worse, and we grow alarmed for the future of our children and grandchildren. But why?

Anxiety does its worst damage especially when all supply lines get cut off—economically, physically, spiritually, relationally. But God has promised manna in those anxious times too. He visits you in the desert of your anxiety and offers peace at just the right moment and in just the appropriate amount. He not only transcends the boundaries of time, He changes and controls the times; not only of all human history but of your life.

That truth alone is manna for your anxious soul. And it ought to usher in a certain peace and calm. You will receive that peace by understanding, by thinking, and by looking at life through the lens of the Word of God and by living in genuine obedience to it. When was the last time you paused and simply opened the Word of God? That's a critical question to wrestle with.

Times are changing, but God is changing the times. You have nothing to fear when God is in such perfect control of the times. You only discover that in the rich and living pages of His Word.

The psalmist David declared, "You have put gladness in my heart, more than when their grain and new wine abound. In peace I will both lie down and sleep, for You alone, O Lord, make me to dwell in safety" (Ps. 4:7–8).

That's manna in anxious times.

So if God is changing the times, and God has made promises to provide daily manna for you *regardless* of the times, then you can sleep at night. Jesus Christ is the same yesterday, today, and forever. He does not change. The times may change, but He does not.

When I think about that, my anxiety level goes way down, my heart beats normally. I feel at peace. And I can relax because God can change the times.

4. God Has Ordained All the Times in Your Life.

The big-picture perspective is that God maintains perfect control over it all. But how does that truth impact your life in more practical ways?

Stop for a moment and consider the things that were causing you anxiety yesterday and perhaps still have you by the throat today. Maybe you thought, *I have this deadline, or this impossible situation right now in my life, and if I don't have a well-timed help, I don't know if I can make it.* Think honestly and specifically about those things that cause you the most frequent and intense periods of anxiety. Now bring all those things under the authority of God's Word.

Consider that He existed before all time, created time, is unrestrained by time, and sovereignly controls all time. Consider that every moment of your past and every second of your future is preordained by Him.

God has ordained that you should trust Him at this particular moment in time, and in this particular situation in which you find yourself. David affirmed this truth when he sang, "Your eyes have seen my unformed substance; and in Your book were all written the days that were ordained for me, when as yet there was not one of them" (Ps. 139:16).

How's that for manna? You've not lived one day that has not had the benefit, provision, and protection of God's gracious providence and care.

God knew about the circumstances that created your anxiety today before the foundations of the world. Before you showed up on an ultrasound, when you were a sperm and an egg, God knew you. He already had a plan for your life that included this day and the circumstances that have caused your anxious thoughts.

This time in your life unfolds fully under His watchful eye, and the moments are being guided gently by His caring hand. He created you. He knows that you are but dust. He knows you better than you know yourself. And while no one is exempt from trials, of this you can be certain: your times (including whatever is causing you the greatest anxiety) are in His hands. God already has a well-timed help in mind for you. Again David declared, "But as for me, I trust in You, O LORD, I say, 'You are my God.' My times are in Your hand" (Ps. 31:14–15).

If your times were in the hands of someone else—a committee, a boss at work, a spouse, a judge—things would be different. But they are not. You exist purely by His will, and the thing that is stressing you and robbing you of sleep belongs to Him. He already has a solution in place, even though you don't see it.

God is the master over your boss; He is sovereign over your situation. He is Lord over your times. He owns your diagnosis. He rules your past and reigns over your future. And you are simply showing up to find out how He is going to give you manna in the morning.

You need to work hard; you need to plan; you need to listen and be open and teachable. But at the end of the day, you need to sleep. A man who considers these things is a man who can sleep. Go to sleep and know that He will be up all night.

5. God Will Take Time to Do the Most Good in Your Life.

The Lord owns time, He appoints time, and He does a good work through time. The reason we men find ourselves in these dicey situations is because God is continually moving us to trust Him. It's all about trust. And He uses the wilderness to teach it.

John Calvin once said, "The human heart is an idol

factory." You may not be worshipping graven images, but you might be worshipping your job. Or your investment portfolio, or your house, or your kids. None of that may seem all that bad, but sometimes men turn those things into gods and trust in those things to give meaning or to get them through their tough times. There is nothing wrong with those things. A wise man saves up for his children and his children's children. That is good stewardship. We are commended for being hard workers and providers for our families. But we cross the line when we start trusting in those things instead of relying on the Lord.

David declared, "But as for me, I trust in You, O LORD" (Ps. 31:14). Why can God be trusted? Because your times are in His hands.

God takes time to do you the most good. Note the wise words of Obadiah Sedgwick: "Providence is pleased to take time before it does us good . . . although [God] does intend a mercy to us, yet He does not always perform it presently. . . . He often delays us when He does not intend to deny us."[2]

And you can be certain that He will get you through daily as He is doing that good work. Perhaps all you have left in your account is $1.17! Yet your God has promised you daily provision. You may hope for *immediate* deliverance from your difficulties. And that is possible, as we'll see shortly. But there may be a greater deliverance and a wider purpose that God intends.

Recently I was out running errands and my wife called

and asked me to pick up some bananas for her protein shakes. When I walked into the local Walmart, I found loads of bananas. Bananas upon bananas were everywhere. But people were walking right past them because they were completely green. I didn't buy any either. Mary didn't want green. She wanted yellow bananas with a little green up around the stalks. She wanted something she could eat that day, but that would also last a few days.

Timing is everything when it comes to bananas. Timing is everything when you are in need of God's help.

So often we are waiting and wondering why God hasn't answered our pressing need. God never sends us a deliverance that is green. When He answers, His provision is not only right, it is ripe.

A premature deliverance is not what is best. He knows what He is doing in your life. A well-timed deliverance is all about timing—never early and never too late. Just in time.

If the Lord is taking time, it is to do you more good. And you have to trust Him with that. It will be there. Manna is always there. Right on time. But right on God's time. And it was Obadiah Sedgwick who also noted that when necessary, God has no problem in hastening the time. When you own time, you can do whatever you want with it.

6. God Hastens the Times.

While God may delay a particular deliverance, there are also times when He will speed up His deliverance.

During a particularly dark time for Israel, God revealed

what He would do for His people through His prophet Isaiah: "All your people will be righteous; they will possess the land forever, the branch of My planting, the work of My hands, that I may be glorified. The smallest one will become a clan, and the least one a mighty nation. I, the LORD, will *hasten* it in its time" (Isa. 60:21–22, emphasis added).

God has the power to speed up history.

If you're like me, you run your life, plan your actions, and devise your business moves according to a certain time schedule. You and I as men can look at what appears to be the normal course and seasons of life and simply take for granted that this is how our lives are going to look. You may assume that you should be at a certain point and have reached a certain income level or standard of living. That's the natural train of thought. Yet unforeseen circumstances enter your life and gum up the whole deal. All of a sudden you're looking through clouds into a very uncertain future.

There may be a job layoff, right at the time of life when companies are only hiring guys much younger than you. The stock market may have plummeted and taken with it all of your retirement investments. You may find a lump in your arm that turns out to be cancer. There are all kinds of unforeseen circumstances in life that can easily and quickly set you back on your heels.

By the way, there has never been and never will be such a thing as financial security. Have you ever sat down with a financial adviser and drawn up a chart outlining what you must accumulate before you retire? It can be scary when it dawns on you that if you are going to retire at a reasonable level of living you will have to save $17,000 a week.

The point is, all that looks absolutely impossible. You and I think about things like that all the time, don't we? We become anxious that we are getting older and our energy is diminishing, and we have no idea how we are going to live after we can no longer pull the weight in our field of work.

When our plans are derailed and our fortunes are reversed, we can be tempted to look anxiously into the future and wonder how we'll make it. The truth is that we are going to need well-timed help. We don't need to know how it is going to happen. We need to know who is going to make it happen. And that's God's specialty.

Manna.

Sometimes we look at our lives and say, "I am behind schedule. And there's no way I can make up the time." But God can hasten the time. In Joel 2, God said, "Then I will make up to you for the years that the swarming locust has eaten, the creeping locust, the stripping locust and the gnawing locust" (v. 25).

Martyn Lloyd-Jones once said, "Locusts can come year after year after year and destroy the crops. If you have lost ten years' worth of crops to locusts, God can give you back those ten years in one year."[3]

The Lord hastens the time. You may be way behind, but God is able to speed up time in His choosing.

In John 6, between the feeding of the twenty thousand and Jesus' claim that He is the Bread of Life, there is a remarkable account that illustrates the Lord's ability to hasten time. One day the disciples depart from shore without Jesus onto the Sea of Galilee.

> Now when evening came, His disciples went down to the sea, and after getting into a boat, they started to cross the sea to Capernaum. It had already become dark, and Jesus had not yet come to them. The sea began to be stirred up because a strong wind was blowing. Then, when they had rowed about three or four miles, they saw Jesus walking on the sea and drawing near to the boat; and they were frightened. But He said to them, "It is I; do not be afraid." So they were willing to receive Him into the boat, and immediately the boat was at the land to which they were going. (vv. 16–21)

Have you ever rowed three or four miles—not in calm water, but in a storm? These guys were getting fatigued. They were running out of resources. They needed well-timed help.

By the way, did you catch that detail at the end of John's account? *Immediately.* Immediately they had made it to their destination. One moment they were four miles out from the land and the next second the boat was on the shore! They couldn't believe their eyes. They were utterly and absolutely astonished at what the Lord Jesus had just done for them. That's power. That's provision. That's manna.

Maybe you feel like that is your life. No matter what you try, you can't make headway. You're rowing as hard as you can against the press of everything—a downsized economy, a shrinking job market, the uncertainty of your health, a seemingly hopeless marriage, the relentless march of time and aging—that's a lot to row against, especially if you're already depleted because you've been in that press for a long time. I wrote this book to tell you that you may be exactly where the Lord wants you to be. Out of resources. Emptied of energy and ideas. Ready for manna. He wants you to trust Him.

In John's story, these disciples were four miles out and running out of energy, rowing hard against the storm. And that's when the Lord showed up. Not too soon and not too late. Right on time. And immediately the situation changed.

They got where they needed to be. Immediately. Not on their own power, but completely by His.

God is not limited by time. He is not impeded by storms or any opposing forces. He is not limited by space. He is God. It doesn't matter what your situation is, or if you're only four miles out with twenty to go; He can get you caught up—immediately.

Manna.

7. God Takes Time, but He Doesn't Waste Time.

God will never waste your time. Sedgwick's pen makes the point, "Although God does take time, yet He will not waste time."[4] Why is it that so often in Scripture you read the word *wait*? Men typically don't want to wait. But often God wants you to wait. Not stall or be idle, but wait for Him.

As God takes time to do us good, we can easily get fatigued and worn out from the wait. Men can quickly get overwhelmed in the struggle just to survive. And when the supply lines get cut off, we begin to lose our hope. The great danger as we wait comes when we lose heart. Yet the apostle Paul said, "Let us not lose heart in doing good, for in due time we will reap if we do not grow weary" (Gal. 6:9).

He is working when you are wearing down. He is fueling His engines when you are running near empty. You're ready to put it in park and He's about to engage. Just wait. Because when He does engage, you'll know it. And everything will look different in the morning.

While you are waiting for His timing, He is working on your behalf. That's the fact of Isaiah 64:4: "No eye has seen any God besides you, who acts on behalf of those who wait for him" (NIV).

And if the answer you desire doesn't come, even that is a good thing. Sometimes our requests are never realized because in His wisdom He knows it is not for our good. The old Puritan pastor summed it up (and I'm paraphrasing from memory here) when he said, The Lord has answered every request I ever made in prayer. He either gave me what I asked or what I should have asked.

You can trust His timing *and* His wisdom.

5

RED LEATHER CHAIR

"My soul languishes for Your salvation;
I wait for Your word."

—Psalm 119:81

The Lord sent the manna, but He didn't serve them breakfast in bed.

Every day God provided the manna to the people of Israel. But they had to get up and get it. They had to collect it, eat it, chew it carefully, swallow, and digest it.

And we must do the same thing with the Word of God. It is our spiritual food and its nutrients are life-giving and essential. Therefore, we must collect it, read it, and digest it.

Meditation is to the soul what food is to the body. To meditate biblically is to consider, to think, to ponder. It means to chew something over in your mind. Psalm 1:2 says, "In His law he meditates day and night."

I met Bill Kennedy a few months ago. He was coming to our Wednesday night men's study here in Dallas and then attending a second men's study I taught in another part of Dallas the very next day. I couldn't imagine anyone coming to hear me teach two days in a row every single week. I sure wouldn't do that. But there he was, week after week. One day he came up to me afterward and introduced himself.

"I've been noticing you at both studies. How long have you been coming?"

"Oh, about a year since I got back to Dallas."

"Where were you prior to coming to Dallas?" I asked.

"I was in prison for seventeen years."

"Really?"

"Yeah, I was in prison."

"Wow."

"Yeah. You know, I was in prison for something I didn't do."

He began to tell me his story and about a man who had helped him get through that difficult time. It was the teacher and author Tim LaHaye, who had been his friend when it all came down. Years ago LaHaye wrote a book called *How to Study the Bible for Yourself*, and in it he spoke about Bill Kennedy's unfortunate situation:

My friend Bill Kennedy was sentenced to 20 years in prison for a crime he never committed. The whole thing is such a confusing malfeasance of justice that it is hard to believe. I am convinced a liberal prosecutor went after Bill with all the power of the government because he was the publisher of one of the most conservative magazines in the country. Liberals didn't like the way he exposed some of their prominent spokesmen and set out to destroy him. Had it not been for the Lord, they would have succeeded. By the time you read this, hopefully his unfair trial will have been overturned and he will be a free man.[1]

It was never overturned, and he ended up serving the full seventeen years.

LaHaye continued:

Whether free or not, he is already a much stronger Christian with a vibrant testimony, even in prison. . . .

The first night Bill called [from prison], I prayed for wisdom in dealing with him. He was understandably very depressed. As gently as I could, I challenged him to begin a Bible study program while in prison that would help him mature in his Christian life. Like many long-term Christians, he was a good father and husband, but very immature spiritually, and he knew it. Obviously, discipling him would be different from most of the men I have discipled through the years. For one thing, I could not call him; he had to call me. I travel a great deal, and he only had limited funds for long-distance calls. The only answer was for me to suggest some tools for Bible study and for Bill to disciple himself.[2]

LaHaye urged him to read the Bible every day, starting with the book of Philippians. This little book, often called "The Epistle of Joy," was written by Paul when he was imprisoned in Rome for his faith. It was the perfect book for Bill to read as he entered his long road of incarceration. In fact, LaHaye suggested he read Philippians every day. Every day! That was a great suggestion for Bill because when Paul wrote Philippians he was in jail for something he didn't do.

Bill said to me, "Let me tell you what happened. I was so depressed when I got in there, I didn't think I could live. I didn't think I could survive. I asked God to save my life and give me the gift of joy." And that is what happened. Joy showed up and filled his heart. But joy didn't just show up as an emotion. It came through the power of the Word of God. It came through reading the inspired Scriptures and pondering the truth, considering the truth, and applying it to his circumstances.

Do you know what is interesting? The whole time he was in this white-collar prison he was leading men to the Lord. They would look at him and see the joy in his life. They couldn't figure it out. Bill had a longer sentence than any other inmate. It just didn't make sense to the other men. They'd come to him and ask, "What is it with you? How do you get the joy?" And Bill would tell them.

There are four other men who attend the weekly Bible

studies I lead who were also imprisoned falsely for white-collar crimes. These are stellar men who spent hundreds of thousands of dollars in legal fees fighting the charges. But like Joseph, they found themselves in prison for crimes they didn't commit. They have all served their time and today are all in the process of watching the Lord direct their steps. Each of them has a significant ministry to other men in similar straits. They are using the manna grace they received they are using to minister to others. They are being used by God but in ways they never imagined. Second Corinthians 1:3–6 describes how it works:

> Blessed be the God and Father of our Lord Jesus Christ, the Father of mercies and God of all comfort, who comforts us in all our affliction so that we will be able to comfort those who are in any affliction with the comfort with which we ourselves are comforted by God. For just as the sufferings of Christ are ours in abundance, so also our comfort is abundant through Christ. But if we are afflicted, it is for your comfort and salvation; or if we are comforted, it is for your comfort, which is effective in the patient enduring of the same sufferings which we also suffer.

God fed these men a special kind of manna out of His Word in that wilderness. And each of them in turn is helping other men learn the importance of feeding daily on God's Word.

JESUS' WILDERNESS EXPERIENCE

It is remarkable to consider that the Son of God spent time in a literal wilderness. Our Lord experienced every wilderness known to mankind. He knew what it was to live hand to mouth ("foxes have holes and the birds of the air have nests, but the Son of Man has nowhere to lay His head" [Matt. 8:20]). He knew the oppression of living under tyranny, as the Israelites had known in Egypt and countless believers have known since then. He grieved over the sickness and death of people who were close to Him. As the multitudes thronged after Him, He carried a burden of responsibility too heavy for any one human being. Daily He endured the scoffing of the religious leaders of His day and evaded their traps. He underwent the humiliation of public rejection and the greater hurt of abandonment by His closest friends. He endured the mockery of several trials and final execution for crimes He did not commit. Whatever wilderness you find yourself in, Jesus understands. For "we do not have a high priest who cannot sympathize with our weaknesses, but One who has been tempted in all things as we are, yet without sin" (Heb. 4:15).

But it was His forty days in a literal wilderness that teaches us His *secret* for survival through His time here on earth. Matthew, Mark, and Luke tell us that after Christ's baptism and before His ministry kicked off, Jesus was led into the wilderness by the Spirit. Mark put it this way: "The Spirit *impelled* Him to go out into the wilderness. And He was in the wilderness forty days being tempted by Satan" (1:12–13, emphasis added). Each account tells us, "After He had fasted forty days and forty nights, He then became hungry" (Matt. 4:2).

He became hungry. What an understatement. I am ready to sell my birthright after being on a diet of lean meat and vegetables for forty days! Jesus had had *nothing* to eat at all. So, yes, He was extremely hungry and in a vulnerable, weakened state. We cannot forget that our Lord was fully man and fully God; it is one of the great mysteries of the Christian faith. That means that He endured the difficulties of life just like we do. He had to eat and sleep just like we do. He required friends and companionship just like us. And just as His countless miracles and wondrous deeds could not all be recorded (John 20:30), neither could all of His trials and sufferings. He was tempted in *every* way that we are tempted. To make matters worse, throughout His days in that literal wilderness, Satan was continuously hassling Him and attempting to break Him down (Luke 4:2). Now watch closely because here comes the secret of surviving in your wilderness.

At the forty-day mark, Jesus reached His weakest moment. So Satan came in for the kill. "Turn these stones into bread," the Devil taunted. This is where we get a glimpse of our Lord's secret. He turned to Satan and quoted from the Old Testament: "It is written, 'MAN SHALL NOT LIVE ON BREAD ALONE, BUT ON EVERY WORD THAT PROCEEDS OUT OF THE MOUTH OF GOD'" (Matt. 4:4).

Satan was taunting Jesus to abandon His servant path to the cross. He was saying, "Take matters into Your own hands. You don't need to depend on Your Father."

Then Satan took Him to the pinnacle of the temple of Jerusalem, and next to a high mountain from which could be seen the kingdoms of the world, he offered Jesus the glory and power of reigning over them all—if Jesus would worship him. Our Lord continued to counter him by quoting from the Scriptures. Finally Satan threw in the towel and left (Matt. 4:11). We are told that then the angels came and ministered to Jesus. Just as an angel fed Elijah in the wilderness, carrying him through a forty-day fast (1 Kings 19:5–8), the angels came and fed Jesus. They brought to Him literal manna from heaven.

What did Jesus mean when He said that a man must live not only by physical bread, but "on every word that proceeds out of the mouth of God"? He was saying that yes, we must eat physical food. But if we are to survive in the wilderness, we must eat spiritual food. *The manna of God's words keeps us alive in every area of our lives. It strengthens us, directs us, comforts us, and gives us wisdom. God's words are soul manna. They are the food that keeps us alive in the wilderness.*

Now, Jesus was not speaking hypothetically. He lived this out all His days. He knew the Scriptures so well that He could quote from them verbatim, and often did. Only a man who reads and meditates regularly on God's words can do that. He knew that Moses had survived two forty-day fasts while in the presence of God in the wilderness (Ex. 24:18; 34:28). Jesus was not the first.

He also knew He was the Messiah promised to Abraham, Moses, and David, and spoken of by the prophets. Yet, though He was God in the flesh, the great "I AM," in becoming a man, He had chosen to lay aside His privileges as God and taken on the form of a servant, humbly dependent on the Father (Phil. 2:6–8). He was the Lamb of God, come to die on a cross as the sacrifice for mankind. Our Lord's incarnation and servant life on earth were taken directly from Scripture. Even as a boy when His parents found Him discussing the Scriptures with the religious leaders in the temple of Jerusalem, He said, "Did you not know that I had to be in my Father's house?" (Luke 2:49). Jesus saw Himself written across the pages of Scripture.

In the wilderness Satan was attempting a preemptive move to take Jesus out before His public ministry ever began. And Jesus knew what he was up to. This is why, even in the Lord's weakened physical state, He rebuked him with the Word of God.

If the Lord Jesus needed the Word of God in His wilderness, why would you think you can make it through yours without the Scriptures?

When you are in the wilderness, you are in a great battle for your heart and mind. Hebrews 4:12 states the fact of its power that cannot be defeated: "For the word of God is living and active and sharper than any two-edged sword, and piercing as far as the division between soul and spirit, of both joints and marrow, and able to judge the thoughts and intentions of the heart."

Not only did the Bible shape our Lord's life on earth, it shaped His ministry to others. He used Scripture to explain, rebuke, comfort, and train those around Him. He used it with the multitudes. He used it with the religious leaders. He used it with the twelve disciples. You could say that Jesus bled Scripture. In the gospel of Matthew alone, we find Jesus directly quoting from the Old Testament seventy-six times. Thirty-three of those quotes were from the Pentateuch: three from Genesis, seven from Exodus, six from Leviticus, one from Numbers, and sixteen from Deuteronomy. Nine times Jesus also directly quoted from Psalms and Proverbs. He quoted from all of the Major Prophets (Isaiah, Jeremiah, Ezekiel, Daniel), and from eight of the twelve Minor Prophets.

Even when He wasn't directly quoting the Old Testament, He was often referring to the people, teachings, and ideas of the Old Testament. Our Lord not only believed the Scriptures to be true but He lived, breathed, and ministered from them.

How astonishing that during His days on this earth, Jesus—the one who *gave* the Word, the one who *was* the living Word Himself (John 1:1)—fed upon the Word. He knew, as Moses taught the children of Israel, that it was His very life.

Deuteronomy 32:46–47 instructs us, "Take to your heart all the words with which I am warning you today, which you shall command your sons to observe carefully, even all the words of this law. For it is not an idle word for you; indeed it is your life."

Jesus' example should make us stop and think. If our Lord lived off of Scripture, how much more do we need to do the same! It is not an idle word. It is your life.

The Word of God contains our amino acids, our vitamins, and our minerals. It contains everything we require in order to maintain mental, emotional, and relational health and strength. We cannot live without this food from God. It is the light and wisdom that exposes our sins and helps us overcome them. It is our sword of defense against the attack of the enemy. It instructs and equips us for all of life.

We may think we can get along without it, but when a man does not feed his soul, he begins to wither away and lose his bearings. Soon he will find himself wandering in a dreary desert of his own making, far away from the Lord of life. Years ago, in my book *Point Man*, I wrote of the dangers of Christian men becoming either spiritually anorexic or bulimic. The problem is still epidemic and deserves another look.

ANOREXIC MEN

We tend to think that anorexia is a female problem. But if you walk into any gathering of Christian men, you will find a roomful of anorexic men. A guy can weigh three hundred pounds and still be severely anorexic. Let me explain.

The first time I ever heard of "anorexia nervosa" was when Karen Carpenter died. If you are from my generation, then you know all about her. If not, just do a Google search of Karen Carpenter. She and her brother were quite a musical team during the late sixties and seventies. She was a beautiful young girl, extremely gifted. He was the writer and she was the brilliant drummer and singer. But at the height of their success, friends began to realize that Karen was starving herself. Even though she was thin, when she looked in the mirror she would see someone grotesquely overweight. Nobody thought she was overweight, but she did. When a person is anorexic, she develops an aversion to food and literally does not eat. The thinner she becomes, the less she eats and the more her body wastes away to skin and bones. Eventually the lack of nutrients sends her body into a crisis. At the age of thirty-three, Karen Carpenter died of a heart attack brought on by her anorexia.

It is possible for a Christian man to be spiritually anorexic. When I did my dissertation at Dallas Seminary in the early 1990s, I surveyed one thousand men across the country. I asked them all kinds of questions about their relationship with Christ, their marriages, their work, their view of the Bible, their ethics. One of the questions I asked was this: "How often do you spend personal time in the Word of God on a weekly basis?" Half of them said that they interacted with the Bible on a personal basis one time a week or less. These were Christian guys. Guys who said they love Christ.

A number of years ago George Gallup did a poll of evangelical Christians. He was shocked at the amount of neglect of the Word of God among evangelicals. He said, "Americans revere the Bible, but by and large, they don't read it."[3] This can easily happen with Christian men. We can revere the Bible and yet never feed upon it in our own personal lives. Then we wonder why we are overwhelmed, confused, and defeated so much of our lives. If you are not interacting with or personally feeding from the words of God, you are slowly starving yourself. You are becoming dangerously malnourished in your soul and spirit.

In the first Gulf War, General Norman Schwarzkopf was leading our troops toward Baghdad. Our tanks moved quickly across the desert in a hundred-hour offensive drive. In the midst of this battle, we began to see news clips of hundreds of Iraqi soldiers coming out of foxholes and ditches, hands held high in surrender. They were emaciated. They were malnourished. They were bowing to American soldiers. These soldiers of Saddam Hussein were giving up right and left. It turned out all their supply lines had been cut off for weeks. The guys were starving. And when a man starves, he won't fight. He has no physical strength and no will to defend himself or his cause. A physically malnourished soldier has no heart, no motivation, and no energy. He becomes red meat for the enemy.

That is also true spiritually.

It should not surprise us then when Christian men come under attack and surrender easily to the enemy of their souls.

Convictions quickly implode in a starving man. Psalm 1:1–3
declares,

> Blessed is the man who does not walk in the counsel
>   of the wicked . . .
> But his delight is in the law [or words] of the LORD,
> And in His law he meditates day and night.
> He will be like a tree firmly planted by streams of
>   water.

We are prone to wander, aren't we? And as we walk
through the world, we are surrounded by powerful, corrupt-
ing influences. It is little wonder that we so easily succumb
when we are not being nourished from the Word of God. It
takes inner strength and wisdom from the daily manna of
God's words to go upstream against the powerful flow of
the world.

BULIMIC MEN

There's a second eating disorder called bulimia. Bulimia
is called the "binge-purge syndrome." A person will eat,
but before they are able to digest the food, they will go to
a restroom, put their finger down their throat, and vomit
up the food, therefore robbing their body of the nutrients.
This is just as dangerous as anorexia, another slow way of
suicide.

This also has a spiritual aspect. When a man is a hearer of the Word but not a doer of the Word, he becomes bulimic.

The words of God have not been given to simply provide knowledge, as important as knowledge may be. They were meant to take us from ignorance to knowledge, and then from knowledge to obedience. Scripture is worthless to you if it enters your mind but never permeates your heart or infuses your will. We don't want just knowledge; we want obedience.

Did you notice that word *meditate* in Psalm 1? "And in His law he meditates day and night" (v. 2). To meditate is to chew on something throughout the day, as a cow chews its cud. It is to bring to mind God's words again and again in the midst of walking through the world. Meditation on God's words involves digestion. And as you chew on and digest it, you are strengthened by its wisdom and perspective. When the mind-set of the world hits you on every side, you are able to stand. And when temptation pulls at you, you have the wherewithal to fight.

The Pharisees had more biblical knowledge than most of us have in our little fingers, but they did not understand or obey it. Jesus called them out on this and charged, "You hypocrites, rightly did Isaiah prophesy of you: 'THIS PEOPLE HONORS ME WITH THEIR LIPS, BUT THEIR HEART IS FAR AWAY FROM ME'" (Matt. 15:7–8).

Then turning to the crowds, He said, "It is not what enters into the mouth that defiles the man, but what proceeds out of the mouth, this defiles the man" (Matt. 15:11).

Jesus was saying the words that come out of our mouths come from our hearts. And what is in our heart is a result of what we feed it. If the words of God go into our brains but never penetrate our hearts or embolden our wills, they are worthless to us. God's words are given to be heard *and* obeyed. They are meant to affect where our feet go, what our hands do, what our eyes feast upon, what our brains ponder, and what comes out of our mouths. A man's choices come straight out of the desires of his heart. Feed and cultivate your heart with wisdom and truth, and you will desire the will of the Lord. You will find the strength to make wise choices. This is how a man survives in the wilderness.

The old saying is true: we really are what we eat.

RED LEATHER CHAIR

A few years ago I was having breakfast with a young pastor on a Saturday morning of a men's conference. He asked me a simple question: "How do you live your life?" He was deadly serious. I asked him to explain his question. "Well, I mean, how do you travel and do all the things you do, and still keep your marriage going and stay connected to your kids?" It was a good question. As I chewed the bite in my mouth, I pondered my reply. I know many men who are brilliant multitaskers, but I am not one of them. They possess the ability to survive on a shockingly small amount of sleep and they can carry off ten times more than I can on a regular basis. I look at them and marvel. I just don't have that ability. I am extremely limited in what I can handle, more limited than most of you who are reading this book. I am a "one or two baller," as they say. So the challenge to live a balanced life is a big one for me. My wife and kids would tell you this. But his question deserved a thoughtful answer.

"I live my life out of a red leather chair," I said.

He blinked puzzlingly.

"With a black leather Bible," I added.

Let me briefly explain what I then explained to him.

When I get up in the morning, the house is quiet. The world is asleep, and the silence is so pervasive I can almost hear the grass growing outside our windows. Because our house is unusually long and narrow, it turns into a tunnel of sacred silence in those early-morning hours. I get my coffee, grab my black leather Bible, and sit in my red leather chair in the living room. That's how I start my day.

That chair is nearly twenty years old and it's got some scars on it. I call it red, but I think the actual color is oxblood. Which kind of fits because over the years, I've spilled just about everything on that chair except oxblood. It's got a few black marks on the arms from my Sharpie pen that will never come out of the leather. But that chair is well built, and I expect to be in it for many more years, Lord willing.

That chair is the cockpit of my life. I run my life out of that chair. I set the course for my day out of that chair. I read my Bible in that chair and I pray in that chair. Sometimes I get on my knees and rest my arms on that chair as I pray.

That red leather chair is more than a chair; it is an altar where I bow and do business with the Lord. You could say it is where the Lord brings me daily manna.

Tucked inside my Bible is a tattered calendar, the *Robert Murray M'Cheyne Bible Reading Calendar*. I have worn out several copies of that calendar over the years. It lays out four chapters to read each day, from four sections of the Bible. That's good because then I don't get stuck in Leviticus reading about the sacrifices and fall asleep. I can be reading a psalm or a chapter of Proverbs, or a portion of Old Testament history, and a couple of places in the New Testament, all in one day. If I read from this calendar each day, I can get through the Bible in a year. I started this when I was in my early thirties. It is kind of shocking to me that I've been doing that now for over thirty years. I don't say that to boast. I only mention it because I realized back then that I'd better get serious about the Bible if I was going to become a mature man in Christ.

There are times when I am on the road and my chair becomes a corner bench in a hotel restaurant, or an airplane seat (with headphones in place), or any place where I can pull away from people. I will readily admit that there are times when I occasionally fall behind, which means I have to mark out some extra catch-up time the next week. So even though I can't juggle many balls, this is one ball I cannot do without. It is the first and most important part of my day.

But maybe you're a nighthawk like Al Mohler. Mohler, who is president of Southern Seminary, described his inner rhythms:

Devotional reading for spiritual profit is an important part of the day, and that begins with the reading of Scripture. In terms of timing, I am somewhat unorthodox. My best time for spending time in the Word is late at night, when all is calm and quiet and I am mentally alert and awake. That is not the case when I first get up in the mornings, when I struggle to find each word on the page (or anything else, for that matter).[4]

If you do your best thinking in the quietness of the late hours when your wife and kids are asleep, you're what I call a nighthawk. You work best on the night shift. So roll with that—it's how God wired you.

The time of day that you choose does not matter. Just make a plan and start working your plan. Some guys I know reserve their lunch hours to meet with the Lord in the Scriptures. It's completely up to you and the rhythms of your life. Just set a time that's best for you and the Lord will meet you.

How interesting that our Lord, who was constantly surrounded by the demands of the throngs, would continually pull away from everyone, including His disciples, and go apart to the mountain or the desert, usually in the early mornings and sometimes for hours at a time. He took choice time each day to meet with His Father.

A man cannot go 24/7 without running out of gas. He has to stop and fill up his tank and tune up his engine. Our Lord was no different. He demonstrated the importance of daily time with His heavenly Father.

I learned this habit from my dad who would rise early every day and read his Bible and pray. Sometimes when I was a young boy, I would awaken to find him kneeling beside his chair with his opened Bible before him. And that example became indelibly imprinted on my mind. I knew by watching my dad that this was how a man keeps on walking with the Lord through thick and thin.

There have been a few times that I have laid aside my Bible calendar. One of them was when I went through that deep depression in my early years as a pastor. I found that for a while I could only read from the Psalms. Which was okay. I couldn't have lived without those psalms. The Lord knew my heart, and He fed me manna from the Psalms.

God knows what each of us needs when we are in the wilderness. Sometimes He will use a rich book that speaks to us and feeds us just what we need. But always the manna comes from His Word. Other books can be great, but the Christian man must remember that at the end of the day, he lives "on every word that proceeds out of the mouth of God."

As the years have gone by, I have wrestled with God in that chair. I have been seized with anxiety and fear in that chair. I have grieved in that chair. I have come to that chair in anguish over one child or another. That chair has heard it all. And the Scriptures have spoken to me time and again. I am continually astonished at how I can read the same passage year after year, only to discover that I missed something in previous years—a phrase, a particular history lesson, a promise from the Lord. The Word is new every morning, every year. It's manna.

Perspective is everything, and at such times my perspective is recalibrated and brought into alignment with God's through the ministry of the Word of God. Then there are the dry times—the times when nothing strikes me at all in my reading, or when my relationship with the Lord feels boring and lackluster. Those are the days when I just have to show up and know that in due time, this will also pass. If I keep showing up, so will the Lord.

This is my rhythm. You must find yours. You have to find your time, your place, your method—your "red leather chair." Some guys are in that season of waking up to crying babies and diapers and rushing to work in traffic. Some guys are in a season of traveling extensively, while other guys are working two jobs just to put food on the table. Some guys find themselves by a hospital bed through the wee hours of the night, caring for a sick parent, or wife, or child. Every season of life, every situation of life brings its challenges. But there is always a "red leather chair" somewhere in that season.

Whatever your situation, the challenge is always to carve out that time and work faithfully at keeping it a priority in your life. Many guys simply close their office doors and spend a few minutes alone with the Lord. Others spend their lunch breaks with God. There are numerous ways to find your "red leather chair."

Today there are a hundred tools at your fingers. You can

read through the Bible in two years instead of one. You can take a particular book of the Bible that interests you and read it through ten times.[5]

You can listen to Scripture on your iPod on the way to work. You can download a Bible app, with all its notations on your iPhone or Kindle, so that if you are at the doctor's office or on a plane you can pull it out and carry on. I know one guy who listens to Scripture in the shower. He takes very long showers. Technology has made our feeding upon Scripture immensely available and easy. When you come across a book that sets your mind on truth, or a message series that is just what you need, a click or a download can take you right there. Today, we have no excuse not to be in the Word.

"But I have a hard time understanding the Bible," people often say. It is important to find a good Bible and invest in a few tools to help you in your journey of feeding on the Word. How much did you spend on your TV, your sound system, your home computer? A Bible is a drop in a bucket compared to any of those things. And it will counter the steady junk and even poisonous messages coming your way from all those devices.

If you are just beginning, you may want to start with *The Living Bible*; it is welcoming and easy to grasp. If you are looking for a Bible that is a clear and literal translation, I recommend the new English Standard Version. The notes and cross references alone are worth the price of that Bible. But there are many other good translations. Some guys like to write down the lesson they have learned from a passage.

Some keep a record of their prayers and God's goodness over time. Some guys like to jot down a verse or a promise that speaks to what they are dealing with and literally take it with them through their day. I have often written such verses on three sticky notes: one to put on my mirror where I shave, one to stick in my car as I drive, and one to put by my computer where I work. Once I have read that verse all day long for several days, it begins to lodge in my brain, where I can access it later when I am in great need of it.

Don't be surprised if you have questions or come across something that confuses you. This is totally normal. Every man who sits down to feed from Scripture will have questions. Look at the comments in your study Bible. And if you are still confused, let me encourage you to write down your questions and ask someone you respect who has a little more experience or theological knowledge.

While there are some difficult passages in the Bible, most of Scripture is surprisingly clear and even simple. Scripture is like our God who gave it. It is very approachable and understandable, yet within it are certain mysteries. Just as God is so approachable that we can know Him and walk with Him in close friendship, He is completely "other" and His nature is incomprehensible. He is God. We are human. So it makes sense that in our limited, finite minds we will have questions. It also makes sense that we will never fully grasp certain truths of Scripture until we are in heaven. "Now I know in part, but then I shall know fully just as I also have been fully known," wrote Paul (1 Cor. 13:12).

There is great power in simply reading the words of Scripture.

Lynn K. Wilder told what happened to her entire Mormon family when their twenty-year-old son began to read the Bible.

The summer of 2006, my husband and I mustered the courage to drive two hours away from our largely Mormon community in Utah to attend a non-Mormon church on a Saturday night. That way, no Mormon friends or priesthood leaders could possibly see us. We were paranoid, worried that if someone from Brigham Young University saw me at a non-denominational Christian church, I would lose my ecclesiastical clearance and my job as a professor.

And I would have. Only at BYU would someone lose their academic position for finding salvation outside the Mormon church. Protestant teachings from the Bible run contrary to the doctrine of Mormon "prophets, seers, and revelators."

My colleagues at secular universities would never have believed I could lose my job over religion. I could imagine the conversation.

"You got fired at BYU?"

"Yes."

"Why?"

"Because I decided to follow a different faith."

"No one would ever fire you just for that! You must have done something wrong."

Our son had faced similar dangers. He risked everything—faith, family, friends, girlfriend, college scholarship, respect—by stepping out of Mormon belief. This son stood before a roomful of fellow Mormon missionaries in Florida to say he had been reading the Bible and now believed in a God of grace—meaning he no longer needed to perform the "good works" outlined by the Mormon church in order to be saved. That was a remarkable act of courage for a 20-year-old in Mormon culture. He was deemed unworthy to be a missionary and sent home. He had been willing to face the consequences. I didn't understand how or why. But I began investigating this God he found so compelling.[6]

This courageous young man read the Word of God and for the first time in his life understood the gospel of Jesus Christ. And not only did he come to know the Lord, but so did his parents and siblings. The entire family came to faith—and they came through a son who was hungry for truth, picked up a Bible, and read it.

What power is in the manna of God's Word! No wonder the enemy will fight you at every turn to keep you from it. But greater is He that is within you than he that is in the world. So schedule a time, pick a place, and start reading your Bible. It's manna—it is the Word of Christ, and in it you will find a well-timed help for this very day.

Only the Word of God can nourish you in the wilderness.

6

GETTING THROUGH IT

"Thy word is a lamp unto my feet,
and a light unto my path."

—PSALM 119:105 (KJV)

When I went through a two-year depression in my early thirties, it was the worst time of my life. I had been in the wilderness before, but I had never gone that deep. I thought I would be there forever. I verged on losing hope for my future. What I couldn't see at the time was that period of my life in depression was necessary for what God wanted to do with the rest of my life. I was worried that I had lost my future. What I didn't know was that He was preparing me for my future. It was the most difficult chapter of my life. I now look back on that season with a different perspective.

Here's what I didn't see and couldn't see at the time: that chapter of my life was a major transition, a very necessary transition.

I had my plans and dreams. I had sort of sketched out what I thought my life would be like. When my plans were destroyed and I found myself in an emotional ditch, I didn't know how to get out of it. I thought God had put me permanently on the shelf, but nothing was further from the truth. He was just pulling me off the field for a while and making me sit on the sidelines. I had some things I needed to learn and experience. They weren't pleasant, but they were necessary for what He had in mind for me. In hindsight, that time of depression was a major turning point. The Lord was transitioning me from my plan for my life to His plan for my life. If I could have known that, I wouldn't have been so depressed. But that's how life works.

Most of life is framed with transitions. We transition from college to the workplace, from living with our parents to finding a mate and setting up a home. From being young and ambitious to settling into a disciplined life, from one career to the next. Suddenly you're transitioning into mid-life, and before you know it, thoughts of retirement are dancing in your head. That's another big transition. And then when the time comes for you to retire, you realize you can't. So now the transition is from retirement dreams to the reality of more work. Young, mid-life, or rounding third and headed for home, whatever your place in life, the truth remains—most of life is framed with transitions.

After the exodus, Israel spent forty years in transition too—wandering and waiting on God for the next chapter of His blessing. Yet, in that time, He promised to provide for them and guide them with His own hand. He does that for you as well. He promises to provide for you and guide you in and through life's transitions.

David exclaimed, "The LORD is my shepherd, I shall not want. He makes me lie down in green pastures; He leads me beside quiet waters. He restores my soul; He guides me in the paths of righteousness for His name's sake" (Ps. 23:1–3).

Sometimes He makes us stop what we are doing and lie down. The problem is we don't want to. We want to keep moving on the fast pace of life. We want to achieve our goals and see our plans turn out just as we imagined. And then He interrupts our plans, takes us off the fast track, and makes us lie down. And usually when He makes us lie down, it's in some kind of wilderness. It can be a hospital bed, a cloud of depression that threatens to suffocate us, divorce papers that blindsided us, or a call from the police to say that they have our son (or daughter) in custody.

When those situations or countless others come into our lives and interrupt our plans and objectives, we need to remember that the invisible hand of God is behind them. He is making us lie down. And more than likely, that's something we really don't want to do.

But even when He makes us lie down, He is leading us. David said that the Lord led him beside green pastures, and when you're a sheep, green pastures are what you want in life. Green pastures for a sheep are the good life. But often when the Lord makes us lie down, we look around and don't see any green—all we see is the brown dirt of the wilderness.

During that two-year depression in my early thirties, the Lord made me lie down and I could hardly function. I had never dealt with depression in my life, and suddenly I was in the middle of it. Those years in depression weren't in my plan or part of my goals for my life. I wasn't living the good life; I was living the disappointing life. There were no green pastures that I could see—only the brown dust and grime of the wilderness, and I couldn't seem to get the taste of it out of my mouth.

But day by day He provided the manna I needed. He walked me through that wilderness of depression. He had purposes for me that I couldn't see when He made me lie down. That was a necessary chapter in life. The whole time He was leading me and preparing me for something I knew nothing about. For what He had in mind was not in my plans—but it certainly was in His. I was completely over-whelmed and confused about what had happened to me. But as the psalmist said in Psalm 142:3, "When my spirit was overwhelmed within me, You knew my path." So you may not have a clue how to get out of the wilderness or how to navigate a transition. That's okay—because you're not the shepherd of your life. You're following Him. You may be overwhelmed, sick with worry, and confused about the next step in your life. Stay close to Him—He knows your path.

His hand is on you on the best day of your life, and it is on you on the worst day of your life. He will use both to accomplish His purpose in your life.

Life's transitions are like chapters in a book. Your life is a biography with multiple chapters, each a transition into the next. What that means is you are either entering into a chapter, in the middle of a chapter, or in a chapter that is coming to an end. We have chapters of our lives, but at the beginning of each chapter and at the end of each chapter, you have a transition.

You, like the Israelites in the wilderness, need daily provision and daily guidance when you are in transition. What you need is wisdom to navigate through the passage. Or to put it another way, you're going to need some more manna. You're going to need some more well-timed help.

GOD AS YOUR GUIDE

Once the Israelites had Egypt in their rearview mirror, they were in the middle of a prolonged transition. And that transition included all the harsh uncertainties of a wilderness experience. Weather. Supply lines cut off. No food. Little water. Piercing heat by day, and total darkness by night. All real, but also all metaphors for how some of life's transitions feel. But God was faithful. He never left them to wander alone and without His gracious leading and provision. Exodus tells the story.

Now when Pharaoh had let the people go, God did not lead them by the way of the land of the Philistines, even though it was near; for God said, "The people might change their minds when they see war, and return to Egypt." . . . The LORD was going before them in a pillar of cloud by day to lead them on the way, and in a pillar of fire by night to give them light, that they might travel by day and by night. He did not take away the pillar of cloud by day, nor the pillar of fire by night, from before the people. (13:17, 21–22)

The Israelites were coming out of Egypt. They had plundered the Egyptians (Ex. 12:36). To make them leave quickly, the Egyptians had given them their gold and silver. As they left Egypt, God provided exceedingly for His people to prepare them for a transition. And then in the wilderness transition, He provided both leadership and direction through the day and through the night. This is how God led His people and guided them through the wilderness for forty years.

Do you ever get confused about what the Lord wants you to do? Do you ever wonder, *Should I take that job or not? Should we make that move or should we not? Do I really want to stay in this ministry?*

I like to think about the cloud God used to guide the Israelites. Quite frankly, it cuts through everything. God's plan was really simple. When the cloud moved, they moved. When the cloud stood still, they stood still. In the daytime and in the night. That's how God leads. Simply. Clearly. Consistently.

Now I have a question for you. How do you think God wants to lead and provide for you? Especially in your wilderness? In whatever transition you might be staring in the face right now?

YOUR CLOUD BY DAY, YOUR FIRE BY NIGHT

How do *you* get guidance today? How does God guide *you*? How does God lead *you* when you find yourself in transition or when you're under pressure to make critical decisions? God has promised He will lead you and guide you just as He did the Israelites in the wilderness for forty years. Below are four principles that will help you understand the way God leads you in transition.

He Leads You by His Word.

David, the shepherd king of Israel, was no stranger to transitions. Perhaps more than anyone else in the Bible, this man knew the deserts of his own making. More often than not, David needed direct and clear guidance from the Lord because he was in the desert—at times literally, at others metaphorically because of his sin. Yet David's confidence remained iron clad in the promise of God to lead him. He declared in Psalm 119:105, "Your word is a lamp to my feet and a light to my path."

In that wilderness for forty years, when Israel needed guidance, they looked up and there it was. A cloud by day, a pillar of fire at night. David looked to the Word of God for guidance. There's a similarity, because today when you need guidance, you look up too. You look up from your circumstances and take the Bible in hand.

What was it that the pillar of fire did for them at night? It gave them light so they could see in the darkness. "Your word is a lamp to my feet and a light to my path."

For forty years, the Lord provided manna every day for His people. He gave them protection and peaceful sleep by night. Yet He also gave them guidance. You need both too. You need God's daily sustenance. But you also need wisdom, every day, especially in transition. You need His Word. Like the Israelites, you look up. But we also live life on a spiritual level, and it is the Word of God that sustains us spiritually. And He gives that daily guidance in His Word—the Bible.

Consider some passages in the Bible that reinforce the reliability of God's words to lead you:

In the beginning was the Word, and the Word was with God, and the Word was God. (John 1:1)

The officers answered, "Never has a man [Jesus] spoken the way this man speaks." (John 7:46)

For the word of God is living and active and sharper than any two-edged sword, and piercing as far as the division of soul and spirit, of both joints and marrow, and able to judge the thoughts and intentions of the heart. (Heb. 4:12)

What was from the beginning, what we have heard, what we have seen with our eyes, what we have looked at and touched with our hands, concerning the Word of Life. (1 John 1:1)

> You will make known to me the path of life;
> In your presence is fullness of joy;
> In Your right hand there are pleasures forever.
> (Ps. 16:11)

Those verses together make a point: Jesus is almighty God, the Living Word of God, and He has given us a book that is His written Word.

Don't try to hear His voice anywhere else. You're only going to get it from His Book. "Well, I want to hear His voice speaking to me," you might say. Then pick up your Bible. It is a guaranteed Word from Him.

Every cult in the world claims to hear His voice from a source other than the Bible. Don't make that mistake. Open your Bible, keep it open, and ask Him to open your eyes so you can behold wonderful things from His law (Ps. 119:18). He will do that for you. He's promised to do it. Don't settle for cheap imitations—no matter how "spiritual" they may seem to be.

He speaks to you in His Word—period. He will lead you

and He will guide you through His book. That's guidance. That's leadership.

John Flavel wrote:

> You read that the Word of God is the only support and relief to a gracious soul in the dark day of affliction (Ps. 119:50, 92; 2 Sam. 23:5) and that for this purpose it was written (Rom. 15:4). Nor rules of prudence, no natural remedies can perform for us that which the Word can do. . . . One word of God can do more than ten thousand words of men to relieve a distressed soul.[1]

He Guides You Through the Bad Stretches of Life.

God can speak most clearly and quite specifically through the harshness of life's wilderness. Jeremiah, one of Israel's prophets, declared,

> Thus says the LORD,
> "What injustice did your fathers find in Me,
> That they went far from Me
> And walked after emptiness and became empty?
> They did not say, 'Where is the LORD
> Who brought us up out of the land of Egypt,
> Who led us through the wilderness,
> Through a land of deserts and of pits,
> Through a land of drought and of deep darkness,
> Through a land that no one crossed
> And where no man dwelt?'" (Jer. 2:5–6)

For Israel, the transition from Egypt would test them beyond their wildest imaginations. They were led by God into a barren wasteland of wilderness. It was a land so depleted and so cursed that nobody lived there. Nobody would dare cross it.

Yet that's where God demonstrated His power and desire to lead them. In the roughest period of adversity, *He leads and sustains.* And you may be in one of those bad stretches right now.

You may be looking around and all you see is desert. You see pits. You see drought. No rain has come, and you're staring into total darkness. That happens, but you're shocked because it's not what you anticipated for your life. I know. I've been there too. God is in that transition, and He leads through those bad stretches of life. David's son Solomon wrote,

> Consider the work of God,
> For who is able to straighten what He has bent?
> In the day of prosperity be happy,
> But in the day of adversity consider—
> God has made the one as well as the other
> So that man will not discover anything that will be
>   after him. (Eccl. 7:13–14)

There is going to be a time when you're in the wilderness. And God will lead you through that difficult passage through the promises of His Word.

Again, John Flavel's words are most helpful.

Did God abandon and cast you off in the day of trouble?
    It is true, there have been some plunges and difficulties you have met with, in which you could see no way of escape, but concluded that you must perish in them. . . . (But) He has either strengthened your back to bear, or lightened that burden, or else opened an unexpected door of escape, according to promise (1 Cor. 10:13), so that the evil which you feared did not come upon you.[2]

It can be a relational wilderness. Maybe the fabric of your marriage has worn paper thin. Suddenly you're looking at an empty nest and you're in the transition of rebuilding your life as a couple. It can be a health wilderness that comes from an ominous diagnosis. Perhaps you thought yourself to be the picture of health and fitness. But now your health is threatened and you're in transition. Or there's just bad news at home, or financially you're hanging on with your fingernails, or whatever it might be. These are life's bad stretches.

And though you're in total darkness, God will lead you through those deep disappointments, through the most grievous losses, or through deep financial droughts and debilitating spiritual or emotional tunnels the way He led Israel in the desert. Day by day. Night after night. By powerful and faithful Word.

Puritan pastor Thomas Watson wrote in his masterful book *All Things for Good*:

As the hard frosts in winter bring on the flowers in the spring, and as the night ushers in the morning-star, so the evils of affliction produce much good to those that love God. . . . A sickbed often teaches more than a sermon. . . . Affliction teaches us to know ourselves. In prosperity we are for the most part strangers to ourselves. God makes us know affliction, that we may better know ourselves.[3]

That makes sense. God leads and guides through the bad stretches of your life. That's why you and I don't always experience prosperity. You and I need to grow. We need to mature. And we always grow stronger when we're going uphill.

He Leads Through Disappointing Delays and Frustrating Circumstances.

I got an e-mail from a friend asking for prayer about a situation. There was a deal he had been working on that should have been signed months earlier, and then another department got involved. To my friend, that interruption was the kiss of death. They were having a meeting that week, and it didn't look good. So much was riding on the outcome of that meeting. My friend felt discouraged because of the disappointing delays and the frustrating circumstances.

That's how life works. We view delays and disappointments as annoyances, not as clouds by day or pillars of fire by night, not as the Lord leading and guiding. But often that's just what they represent. Again, consider the wisdom of David in Psalm 119. He exclaimed,

> Forever, O LORD,
> Your word is settled in heaven,
> Your faithfulness continues throughout all
> generations;
> You established the earth, and it stands.
> They stand this day according to Your ordinances,
> For all things are Your servants.
> If Your law had not been my delight,
> Then I would have perished in my affliction.
> (vv. 89–92)

According to the Word of God, those annoying disappointments and delays are the Lord's servants. They help Him lead you. To accomplish His will for you. To guide you. To give you manna in transition.

All circumstances of your life are His servants. He's sovereign over everything. If you're experiencing a delay, that delay is not the master of your life; that delay is under the authority *of* the Master of your life. And you could only discover that while pressing against the bad stretches of life. You're not going to get that anywhere else. In the bad delays of life, you are forced to deal with uncertainty rather than certainty. And that is a heavy weight to carry.

Jon Bloom provided a discerning observation about the reasons for uncertainty in our lives:

Uncertainty is a difficult thing to bear. We want to know where the provision is going to come from or if we're going to die of this disease or how this child is going to turn out or if our job will be there next month.

But Jesus made it clear that his disciples must be able to bear uncertainty if they are to follow him. . . . Can you bear not knowing how God is going to provide for your most urgent needs and still trust that he will?

There are simply going to be times when obedience and faithfulness to his call means we aren't sure where the provision for our needs will come from. Unforeseen circumstances will occur. Plans will fall through. The salary might not allow for much retirement savings. Financial support might need to be raised. A thief may break in and steal. Economies may collapse. Radical generosity may be required to meet another's desperate need. A debilitating illness may befall. Religious or racial discrimination may deny. . . .

Jesus doesn't want us to be governed by fear at such times. He wants us governed by faith. The uncertainty we are faced with is only apparent uncertainty. Our future and our provision and our ultimate triumph are certain to God. . . . Apparently uncertain seasons are often some of the most powerful moments we experience with God in this age. More than seasons of security and prosperity, they demonstrate that God exists and rewards those who seek him (Heb. 11:16).[4]

He Leads Through Wise Advisors Who Know the
Word.

Not only should you get in the Word, but you should
have select advisors in your life who are also people of the
Book. Reflect on some passages from the Bible that help
reinforce this thought.

Proverbs 13:20 says, "He who walks with wise men will
be wise." How did they get wise? The fear of the Lord is
the beginning of wisdom. There ought to be a few choice
people in your life who are further down the trail from you,
who have known the Lord longer, and who have a little more
depth spiritually because of their investment in the Word of
God. They are priceless to you in times of uncertainty and
transition.

Proverbs 15:22 tells us, "Without consultation, plans are
frustrated, but with many counselors they succeed." How
many times have we run off on our own and done something
and never sought counsel from anybody else? We've all done
it, but it's not the best way to live your life. There ought to
be at least two people in your life whom you can check in
with and get their counsel when something major is going
on. Run those actions and decisions through the lens of their
knowledge of and experience with the Word.

Proverbs 11:14 declares that "in abundance of counselors there is victory." If you know some godly people, they
ought to be the people you interact with regularly, especially in times of transition. Why? Because they know the
Word. I have a couple of guys in my life who are steady and

reliable guides for me when I'm in the press. If I have a major decision, I'm on the phone with those guys. Every time. I'm looking for red flags. Even yellow flags.

By the way, my wife is my most reliable advisor. If Mary throws up a red flag, that's a red flag for me. She's not always right, but she has great discernment. Why would I go against a woman who wants my best and is committed to the Word? I've not been perfect in this area. At times I've ignored her concerns. She was always gracious, but I wound up in a ditch.

Solomon taught, "Anxiety in a man's heart weighs it down, but a good word makes it glad" (Prov. 12:25). Every word should be tested to see if it passes the test of Scripture. When it does, grab it. If it doesn't pass, get rid of it.

Have you ever had someone speak a word to you that transformed your perspective, put courage in your heart, and recalibrated your plans? That was a well-timed help. It was manna.

IN QUIETNESS AND CONFIDENCE

A few years back I got that dreaded letter from the IRS: "We're going to do an audit on your ministry." *Fine. Audit us*, I thought to myself. They did. It didn't last long, but then they decided to continue the fun with me personally. That's where it got interesting. That was a three-year ordeal.

God was very gracious to me during that time. I, of course, feared the worst. I could have lost everything. No one wants to go up against the IRS. Your mind and your imagination can go crazy with you, and you could drive yourself insane thinking about all the possible problems. I think it's safe to say that in that whole time, I had two nights where I found it totally impossible to sleep. Still, God was gracious. I would go to bed living off the Word. One morning I woke up, and the first conscious thought I had was, *Isaiah 30.* There was no voice, but the Lord planted a verse in my mind. I was in bed thinking, *Isaiah 30. Isaiah 30. I know Isaiah 40 and 41. What is in Isaiah 30?*

I got up, went into the study, got my Bible, and turned to Isaiah 30. Isaiah 30 recounts the story where the nation of Judah was about to make an alliance with Egypt. Another nation was about to attack them, and they were looking to Pharaoh in Egypt to be their protector and provider and deliverer. Instead of looking at the living God, they were going to a pagan ruler.

Here is what I read that morning: "For thus the Lord GOD, the Holy One of Israel, has said, 'In repentance and rest you will be saved, in quietness and trust is your strength'" (Isa. 30:15). In other words, "You don't need to go to Pharaoh; you need to come to Me."

The word *repentance* contains the idea of returning. Here's my paraphrase: "For thus says the Lord God, the Holy One of Israel, 'In *returning to me* and rest you will be saved; in quietness and trust is your strength.'" As I sat there in my study and pondered this, I decided to look at my commentary on Isaiah by H. C. Leupold.

He wrote, "There are times when you are in such an over-whelming situation and the powers against you are so beyond your ability to fight or defend yourself that all you can do is to cast yourself on the living God."[5] That wise scholar took that verse in Isaiah the Lord led me to that morning and melted it down to three principles. By the way, this could be manna for you as it was for me that morning.

First, *wait calmly.* Don't panic. Trust. God is there, and He is leading you in this transition. Listen to His voice. Watch for His provision.

Second, *remain quiet.* Resist the urge to open your mouth and blurt out your plans. There's a simplicity and a power in being silent before the Lord. Some of us just like to hear the sound of our voices to the point that we can't hear God's. Give Him a chance to speak before taking matters into your own hands.

Third, *maintain confidence.* Look to Him! When fearful thoughts invade your mind, look to Him. Remind yourself of His power, His care, and His oversight of your life. "The LORD will accomplish what concerns me," David said in Psalm 138:8, and He will do the same for you. Your confidence must remain in Him no matter how harsh the elements or how bleak everything appears. He will guide and provide. The manna will be there. You can trust that.

During that wilderness of my audit, I lived off those three principles from Isaiah 30 until the day God delivered me. He kept me going by the power of His Word and the faithful provision of some wise counselors. Those were not easy times. But He led me all the way. And He brought a favorable ruling after those years of waiting. You may be waiting, but He is worth waiting for. And in the interim He has manna to see you through. The Bible is the book that will lead you and guide you no matter what wilderness you're in.

Let's close this chapter with two final observations on guidance.

THERE IS A PROMISE OF GUIDANCE

It is found in Psalm 32:8: "I will instruct you and teach you in the way which you should go; I will counsel you with My eye upon you." That is a flat-out, ironclad promise. Do you want God to counsel you? Do you want God to lead you? He says He will.

But watch this. He wants you to have a teachable spirit. The next verse says, "Do not be as the horse or as the mule which have no understanding, whose trappings include bit and bridle to hold them in check, otherwise they will not come near to you." What won't come near to you? Instruction, counsel, and guidance from God. In other words, God says, "Listen, I will instruct you, I will counsel you, I will teach you in the way you should go, but when I do it, don't you be like some mule."

There is a promise of guidance, but it's only given to those with a teachable spirit. If you're not teachable, you're going to go to summer school until you become teachable and learn the lessons. The promise of guidance is given to those who will listen and obey. If you want God to counsel you and give you guidance, He will give it to you.

Look closely also at James 1:5: "But if any of you lacks wisdom, let him ask of God, who gives to all generously and without reproach." If you're not sure what to do, ask Him, and He will give you wisdom for the next step. He may not give you the next two months or the next three months or the next six months, but He'll give you the logical next step. That is an ironclad promise of guidance.

THERE IS A PREREQUISITE
FOR GUIDANCE

Psalm 32:1–2 says, "How blessed is he whose transgression is forgiven, whose sin is covered! How blessed is the man to whom the LORD does not impute iniquity, and in whose spirit there is no deceit!" This psalm of David's ties in with Psalm 51, where he expressed repentance and great remorse for his sin with Bathsheba.

David was up on his rooftop, saw this beautiful gal down getting into her tub at night, called her, and slept with her. Her husband was one of his mighty men, Uriah the Hittite. Then David got word from Bathsheba that she was pregnant. He decided the best way to cover his tracks was by bringing Uriah back from the front to give him an update and then send him home to sleep with his wife.

Uriah came home, but he did not sleep with Bathsheba. He slept on the front porch. Not even on the couch, but on the porch, the front step, because he said that if his men couldn't be with their wives then he wasn't going to be with his. That guy had character. David had him stay another night, hoping to break him down, but Uriah did the same thing. So David sent him back to battle with instructions to his commanding officers to put Uriah on the front lines. Uriah was of course killed.

Now David was an adulterer and a murderer. After a while, David married Bathsheba. Everyone thought it was a noble thing to do, to give this poor widow a home. But watch how he described these events:

> When I kept silent about my sin, my body wasted
> away
> Through my groaning all day long.
> For day and night Your hand was heavy upon me;
> My vitality was drained away as with the fever heat
> of summer.
> I acknowledged my sin to You,
> And my iniquity I did not hide;
> I said, "I will confess my transgressions to the LORD";
> And You forgave the guilt of my sin. (Ps. 32:3–5)

Eventually David poured out his heart before God (Ps. 51). He was living in darkness, but God brought his sin out into the light. He came clean, and there was forgiveness. My point is the ironclad promise of guidance is preceded by the prerequisite of repentance of known sin.

Thomas Watson used to say that "repentance is the vomiting of the soul." Repentance isn't making excuses or rationalizing what you have done. It is heaving up your sin and purging it from your heart before the living God.

If there is known sin in your life, if there is sin you're coddling, if there is sin you are excusing, if there is sin you are rationalizing, do not ask God for guidance. He has made it very clear what is sin and what isn't. For example, if there is sexual sin you think you're getting away with, let me tell you, it makes no sense to ask for guidance. Why? Because "This is the will of God, your sanctification; *that is*, that you abstain from sexual immorality," if indeed that's what you're in (1 Thess. 4:3).

Does that make sense? It makes all kinds of sense. And then when you come clean, He says, "I will instruct you and teach you in the way you should go" (Ps. 32:8). That's manna—an extremely valuable well-timed help.

Listen to what Augustine prayed. "Without you, what am I to myself but a guide to my own destruction?"[6] By the way, if you know anything about Augustine, he was raised by a godly mother, departed from the faith, lived just a wild, insane life of immorality, and then the Lord began to come after him and brought him back. He says, "Without you, what am I to myself but a guide to my own destruction?" The Lord Jesus is a great Savior. He saves us from our sin, our shame, our own plans, and our stupidity. And then He gives us a desire to follow Him in paths of righteousness. If left to ourselves, we will destroy our lives. But He has rescued us, saved us, redeemed us, and bought us with a price.

And with that much invested, He will make sure to guide us all the way home.

7

LITTLE SINS

"The character of a life is not set in
two or three dramatic moments,
but in 10,000 little moments."

— PAUL TRIPP

Elisabeth Elliot was a woman who knew the wilderness,
disappointment, and hardship. But she also knew her
Bible and believed it deeply. In June 2015, after a ten-year
battle with dementia, Elisabeth was called to enter her eternal reward.

As a young woman, she married Jim Elliot, and together
they reached out to the remote tribes in the jungles of
Ecuador with the gospel. One day Jim and four of his fellow missionaries flew into a remote jungle area to meet with

three tribal leaders. All five were speared to death on the banks of the river. Elisabeth had a ten-month-old daughter when her husband was murdered. For the next several years, she lived with the tribe who murdered her husband and saw the leaders become believers in the Lord Jesus Christ.

She then returned to the United States and met and married seminary professor Addison Lietch. Just months after their marriage, he contracted cancer. He died four years later.

In the next decade of her life, she met a widower named Lars Gren, and after several years of friendship, they became man and wife. They were married for thirty-six years. For the last ten years of their marriage, he was her primary caregiver as she suffered from dementia.

This remarkable woman who influenced so many through her writings and daily radio program had a motto she lived by and passed on to others: "What does the Bible say? Do what the Bible says."

Elliot stopped giving speeches in 2004 as her health worsened. When she realized she was losing her memory, she put into practice what she had long preached: "From acceptance comes peace." Her husband said she turned to the Bible for comfort, especially Isaiah 43:2: "When you pass through the waters, I will be with you; and through the rivers, they shall not overwhelm you; when you walk through the fire, you shall not be burned, and the flame shall not consume you" (NIV).

Gren said Elliot handled her dementia just as she did the deaths of her husbands. "She accepted those things, [knowing] they were no surprise to God," Gren said. "It was something she would rather not have experienced, but she received it."[1]

The trials of the wilderness can be devastating. They can put you in a place of honest confusion very quickly. Why is the pain so great and the crushing so thorough? This is where we must keep our Bibles open to navigate us through the trials and keep hope alive. If we close our Bible and keep it closed, hope will die. If we keep it open, His Word can nourish us with timely manna to keep our hope alive. Psalm 130:5 says it best: "I wait for the LORD, my soul does wait, and in His word do I hope."

When we lose hope, we start thinking wrong thoughts about the Lord. And when we have a wrong perspective on what He is doing in our lives, we can easily lose our ability to give thanks. But when hope is fueled by small doses of Scripture, hope returns, and with it comes a thankful heart, even in the worst stretches of the trial.

Elisabeth Elliot knew great sorrow and grief throughout her life. But she kept her Bible open and kept watch over her attitude toward the Lord's dealings in her life. We would do well to follow that model in our own wilderness.

WATCH YOUR HEART—THE SIN OF COMPLAINING

When we think of the disease of complaining or grumbling, we tend to think of that as a "small" sin. The problem is that those smaller attitudes grow deeper and more chronic over time.

On April 17, 1859, C. H. Spurgeon delivered a sermon to over ten thousand people at the Music Hall in the Royal Surrey Gardens. The title of the sermon was "Little Sins." He said,

> It shall be my business this morning to answer this temptation, and try to put a sword in your hands wherewith to resist the enemy when he shall come upon you with this cry;—"Is it not a little one?" and tempt you into sin because he leads you to imagine that there is but very little harm in it. "Is it not a little one?"[2]

In his sermon, he made four key points about what we consider to be little sins.

1. The best of men have been afraid of little sins.
2. Little things lead to greater things.
3. Little sins multiply very fast.
4. A little sin involves a great principle.

To illustrate the point, he referred to a little packet of seeds that was sent from Scotland to Australia over 150 years ago. That little package created huge problems that cost ranchers and farmers hundreds of millions of dollars annually to this day.

Years ago there was not a single thistle in the whole of

Australia. Some Scotchman who very much admired thistles—rather more than I do—thought it was a pity that a great island like Australia should be without that marvelous and glorious symbol of his great nation. He, therefore, collected a packet of thistle-seeds, and sent it over to one of his friends in Australia. Well, when it was landed, the officers might have said, "Oh, let it in; 'is it not a little one?' Here is but a handful of thistle-down, oh, let it come in; it will be but sown in a garden—the Scotch will grow it in their gardens; they think it a fine flower, no doubt,—let them have it, it is but meant for their amusement." Ah, yes, it was but a little one; but now whole districts of country are covered with it, and it has become the farmer's pest and plague. It was a little one; but, all the worse for that, it multiplied and grew. If it had been a great evil, all men would have set to work to crush it. This little evil is not to be eradicated, and of that country it may be said till doomsday,—"Thorns and thistles shall it bring forth." Happy would it have been if the ship that brought that seed had been wrecked. No boon is it to those of our countrymen there on the other side of the earth, but a vast curse. Take heed of the thistle-seed; little sins are like it.[3]

Spurgeon did not overstate the problem of thistles in Australia. The thistles spread so quickly over the pastures and crop lands that the Thistle Act of 1852 was written into law.

Just like the thistle seeds destroyed the crops in Australia, the seeds of complaining and grumbling took root and choked the hearts and minds of the Israelites. The nation of Israel had just experienced one of the greatest victories ever in the history of the world. They should have been overcome with thankfulness and gratitude to God. But within days, the seeds of complaining and grumbling were taking root and choking their hearts and minds. Little sins were about to do tremendous damage.

God had shown His immense power in bringing them out of the sea and drowning Pharaoh and his approaching army. Exodus 15 actually records a portion of a praise song that was sung to commemorate that great event: "Sing to the Lord, for He is highly exalted; the horse and his rider He has hurled into the sea" (v. 21).

Israel erupted into spontaneous praise for the Lord's powerful and faithful deliverance. That's the only response that makes sense, right? God had led them through that sea on dry land. Then, when Pharaoh's army followed, the clouds descended and confused them, the sea collapsed on them, and the entire enemy was wiped out. That display of God's goodness and power brought about tremendous gratitude and thanksgiving.

However, the thrill of victory soon changed to agony of defeat when food and water were scarce. And within a short period of time, their singing changed to grumbling.

Then Moses led Israel from the Red Sea, and they went out into the wilderness of Shur; and they went three days in the wilderness and found no water. When they came to Marah, they could not drink the waters of Marah, for they were bitter; therefore it was named Marah. So the people grumbled at Moses, saying, "What shall we drink?" (Ex. 15:22–24)

How quickly they forgot.

SHORT-TERM MEMORY LOSS

These people were out of water, yet they experienced God's deliverance. Prior to that, they had seen God send ten plagues on the nation of Egypt. The tenth plague finally convinced Pharaoh to let them go. They were just three days away from a major victory, and they were grumbling. Why? Because they forgot the Lord's goodness.

The whole congregation of the sons of Israel grumbled against Moses and Aaron in the wilderness. The sons of Israel said to them, "Would that we had died by the Lord's hand in the land of Egypt, when we sat by the pots of meat, when we ate bread to the full; for you have brought us out into this wilderness to kill this whole assembly with hunger." (Ex. 16:2–3)

Then in Exodus 17:2 they faced another water crisis, and they again complained and took out their frustration on Moses: "Therefore the people quarreled with Moses."

Now let's get the context. God had brought them from slavery out of Egypt, saved them from Pharaoh's army at the Red Sea, and miraculously given them water and manna each day. And what was their response? They were complaining, grumbling, and whining. Instead of praising God for His mighty acts and trusting Him to help them again as He promised, they begin to indict the Lord God. They made accusations absolutely contrary to the evidence of God's power, care and deliverance. And here is where we will see how quickly the complaining and murmuring revealed like an MRI what was really going on in their hearts.

Larry Richards explained:

Exodus 15:22 through Exodus 18 relates the events that transpired on the Israelites' two-month journey from the Red Sea to Mount Sinai. Reading quickly through it, we garner the impression that the Israelites are a bunch of complainers. They gripe. They grumble. They "contend" with Moses. If you read other English versions, you'll see that they also murmur.

What we don't get from any English version is the significance of this reaction. The Hebrew phrase *lon 'al*, "grumble against," which occurs seven times in five verses in Exodus 16, describe an attitude of bitterness and hostility. The Hebrew verb *marah*, which depicts the people's words and actions in Exodus 15:22–24 and Exodus 16:1–8, describes these Israelites as *rebellious*. Their problem wasn't just a lack of trust. It wasn't simply that they whined a lot. These people bridled; they were totally unwilling to submit to God. Suddenly, unexpectedly, we see the same rebellious attitude in God's people that Egypt's pharaoh displayed![4]

Is it not remarkable how quickly Israel forgot the works of God on their behalf? And the seeds of complaining and resentment spread and grew like wildfire into outright rebellion and stubborn unbelief.

The depth of their hostility toward the Lord is revealed in Exodus 17:2 when the two million people were out of water for the second time. Did they remember the miracle the Lord did the first time to supernaturally supply water just in the nick of time (Ex. 15:22–25)? No, they never gave it a thought. The next water crisis was just weeks later and is recorded in Exodus 17. From the response of the people to the second crisis you would get the impression that God never did a miracle the first time around. But He did provide a well-timed help—and instead of remembering and being thankful, they completely obliterated His goodness from their minds.

All the congregation of the people of Israel moved on from the wilderness of Sin by stages, according to the commandment of the LORD, and camped at Rephidim, but there was no water for the people to drink. Therefore the people quarreled with Moses and said, "Give us water to drink." And Moses said to them, "Why do you quarrel with me? Why do you test the LORD?" But the people thirsted there for water, and the people grumbled against Moses and said, "Why did you bring us up out of Egypt, to kill us and our children and our livestock with thirst?" So Moses cried to the LORD, "What shall I do with this people? They are almost ready to stone me." And the LORD said to Moses, "Pass on before the people, taking with you some of the elders of Israel, and take in your hand the staff with which you struck the Nile, and go. Behold, I will stand before you there on the rock at Horeb, and you shall strike the rock, and water shall come out of it, and the people will drink." And Moses did so, in the sight of the elders of Israel. And he called the name of the place Massah and Meribah, because of the quarreling of the people of Israel, and because they tested the LORD by saying, "Is the LORD among us or not?" (Ex. 17:1–7 ESV)

You might ask why we are looking at this issue of complaining in such detail. Here's the answer from 1 Corinthians 10:9–13:

We must not put Christ to the test, as some of them did and were destroyed by serpents, nor grumble, as some of them did and were destroyed by the Destroyer. Now these things happened to them as an example, but they were written down for our instruction, on whom the end of the ages has come. Therefore let anyone who thinks that he stands take heed lest he fall. No temptation has overtaken you that is not common to man. God is faithful, and he will not let you be tempted beyond your ability, but with the temptation he will also provide the way of escape, that you may be able to endure it. (ESV)

We are told specifically that we are not to grumble as they did. These events of the Israelites in the wilderness were written for our instruction. If you think this doesn't apply to you, you should take heed lest you fall. We are all subject to these terrible sins, but God is faithful to help us escape from the temptation of complaining and grumbling and accusing God as we go through the wilderness.

Philip Ryken noted that they were out of line with God in three different ways:

First they said, Give us water to drink (Exod. 17:2a). The sin here is *demanding God's provision*—not asking or waiting for it, but insisting on it. They were telling God that he had to give them what they wanted or else there was no telling what they might do. In our rebellion we often do the same thing. We insist on having our own way. When God does not do for us what we think he ought to do, in the way we think he ought to do it, we complain about it. At home, at work, and in the church, we demand God's provision on our own terms.

The second thing the Israelites said was, "Why did you bring us up out of Egypt to make us and our children and livestock die of thirst?" (v. 3). Here they were *denying God's protection.* The people assumed the worst, as they usually did, and thus they concluded that God had abandoned them, even to the point of death. Although their words were directed against God's prophet, they were really impugning God's motives. Again, we often commit the same sin. We complain that what God is doing in our lives—especially the suffering we must endure—is not good for us but harmful. This is to deny God's protection.

The third thing the Israelites did was to test God, saying, "Is the Lord among us or not?" In this case, their sin was *doubting God's presence.* The lack of water made them wonder if God was really with them at all. Our own trials often raise the question, "Are you really there, God? If you are, you sure don't seem to be blessing me very much right now!" When we adopt this attitude, we are guilty of denying God's presence.[5]

Now here they were again making accusations against the Lord. How could they forget so quickly?

Attitude. That's how. A grumbling attitude causes you to make accusations against God that have absolutely no factual basis, especially when you can't get relief and the pressure mounts. Proverbs 4:23 says, "Guard your heart, for everything you do flows from it" (NIV). You have to watch your heart, and I have to watch my heart, especially in the wilderness.

You must watch your mind and pay attention to your thoughts, because those thoughts can get away from you, and you can very quickly become irrational in your thinking. Then your mouth starts running, and you start saying things you shouldn't be saying. Eventually, you lose your self-control because you have not kept a guard on your heart.

And if you're like me, as you read this story, you're thinking, *Why doesn't God slam these people?* Yet in the midst of their grumblings and their selective memory and all their irrational accusations that had no basis in fact, God showed mercy and grace and sent the manna. Grace in the wilderness. In the face of a grumbling, complaining people.

Read what God said in retrospect, looking back on that season in Israel's history: "For forty years I loathed that generation, and said they are a people who err in their heart, and they do not know My ways" (Ps. 95:10).

Israel had all these facts about the goodness of God. They had witnessed His power and had become recipients of His wondrous grace and provision. They knew all of this, and God declared in Psalm 95 that the problem was their hearts. They did not know His ways. And they had a rebellious attitude that ignored His purposes and plans.

They refused to remember the evidence of God's goodness and provision that was waiting for them every morning, and in so doing they weren't thankful. It may seem to be a little sin not to be thankful, but their example of complaining and indicting God shows us that is not the sane or rational path to take.

This is what the nation of Israel did. Is that not where the United States of America is? And you can add to the list Canada, Great Britain, and the nations of Europe that once stood for the gospel of Christ.

Abraham Lincoln said, "At what point then is the approach of danger to be expected? I answer, if it ever reach us, it must spring up among us. It cannot come from abroad. If destruction be our lot, we must ourselves be its author and finisher. As a nation of freemen, we must live through all time, or die by suicide."[6] As it happened to Israel, so it has happened to us.

SUPPRESSING THE TRUTH

Because of sin, our nature is to resist God and suppress His truth. He can reveal His will plainly and clearly and reveal the truth about Himself, our situation, and the attitude of our hearts, but we can choose to ignore what He has shown us and done for us. This is especially grievous when God has revealed Himself all around us in the wonder and provision of creation.

The apostle Paul developed this notion in the beginning of his epistle to the church at Rome. He wrote,

---

For the wrath of God is revealed from heaven against all ungodliness and unrighteousness of men who suppress the truth in unrighteousness, because that which is known about God is evident within them; for God made it evident to them. For since the creation of the world His invisible attributes, His eternal power and divine nature, have been clearly seen, being understood through what has been made, so that they are without excuse. . . . They exchanged the truth of God for a lie, and worshiped and served the creature rather than the Creator, who is blessed forever. Amen. (Rom. 1:18–20, 25)

God's people saw His wondrous power enacted on their behalf in the wilderness, but they refused to acknowledge Him. They refused to give Him glory. They suppressed the truth in unrighteousness, and they refused to give Him thanks. That is the nature of the human heart, to suppress the truth of God and exchange it for an unrighteous substitute.

It's what's wrong with our culture, it's what's wrong with our marriages, it's what's wrong with our education system, and it's what's wrong with our own personal lives. Mankind simply refuses to honor and acknowledge the Lord and express genuine gratitude for all He provides and supplies.

And we all know better because of the wisdom of God revealed to all of us since creation. Let me illustrate some principles regarding how God's wisdom is revealed.

There Is a Wisdom Revealed in Common Sense.

"That which is known about God is evident within them; for God made it evident to them" (Rom. 1:14).

You and I possess an innate sense of right and wrong, prudence, and good judgment. It's called common sense. I've sometimes heard *wisdom* defined as "sanctified common sense," which seems right to me. Where does genuine wisdom come from? Solomon declared, "The fear of the LORD is the beginning of wisdom" (Ps. 111:10). That kind of common-sense wisdom comes from God. That means it makes absolutely perfect sense to honor and acknowledge the Creator, the sovereign Lord of the universe. And in having that attitude we gain true wisdom.

In other words, every man knows in his heart of hearts that God exists. God has written the truth of Himself on our hearts.

There Is a Wisdom Revealed in Creation.

"For since the creation of the world His invisible attributes, His eternal power and divine nature, have been clearly seen, being understood through what has been made, so that they are without excuse" (Rom. 1:20).

Study the stars or even simply gaze with wonder into a starlit night and God reveals Himself to you. David declared in Psalm 19 that "the heavens are telling of the glory of God," but "their voice is not heard" (vv. 1, 3).

The universe speaks volumes that there is a Creator. All of revelation concerning God is designed and determined to bring about a response of gratitude and honor, to cause mankind to bow in reverence and submission and worship and thanksgiving. Instead, because our nature is to suppress the truth, we grumble. Especially when life takes uncertain turns.

Paul wrote, "For even though they knew God, they did not honor Him as God or give thanks" (Rom. 1:21). What an indictment! Giving thanks is the opposite of grumbling. Giving thanks is the opposite of complaining and murmuring. It's a rational and appropriate response to the revealed truth of God.

The nation of Israel in the wilderness had evidence of God's goodness within them and all around them in His wondrous and faithful provision. They knew it from the witness of common sense and from the awesome mystery of creation, yet they grumbled against Him. They, in essence, suppressed the truth and exchanged it for a lie.

That's what happens when you refuse to honor God, especially in difficult times. Your thinking becomes twisted. Your attitude becomes irrational. And instead of giving thanks to God and honoring Him for His daily manna, you grumble about not having what you want.

One time I was talking to a Christian guy about his personal struggles. He told me he wanted to show me a picture. He paused, reached into his pocket, and pulled out a picture of a house. I thought he was going to show me a picture of his wife or his kids or grandkids. Instead, he was carrying around a picture of a house he'd owned years earlier. It was a very nice house, a dream house you could say. But he lost it through a financial setback. I was somewhat at a loss for words. It was just a house—concrete slab foundation, wood framing, sheet rock, insulation, brick and shingles—yet he was holding on to the memory of it as if it were a precious treasure.

Robert E. Lee was traveling through a Southern state after the Civil War. He stopped for some refreshment at a large plantation that was still intact. As he got off of his horse, the lady of the house came out and immediately showed him a blackened stump in front of the beautiful home. She began to tell Lee that the stump had been a majestic oak tree until a Northern shell hit it. He listened kindly, but the woman continued to rail on about the greatness, beauty, and majesty of the great oak that the Northern army had destroyed. Her bitterness began to spill out over her grief for the stately tree that had been the centerpiece of the plantation's entrance.

When she stopped speaking to take a breath, Lee looked at her and said, "My dear lady, cut it down and forget about it."

Listen to the discerning words of John Flavel:

Whatsoever we have over-loved, idolized, and leaned upon, God has from time to time broken it, and made us to see the vanity of it; so that we find the readiest course to be rid of our comforts is to set our hearts inordinately or immoderately upon them. For our God is a jealous God, and will not part with His glory to another.[7]

There Is a Wisdom That Once Wholly Ignored Can
Be Lost Beyond Retrieving.

"For this reason God gave them over to degrading pas-
sions. . . . And just as they did not see fit to acknowledge God
any longer, God gave them over to a depraved mind, to do
those things which are not proper" (Rom. 1:26, 28).

If you insist on denying the truth about God and rebelling against His revealed truth and you want to live as though
God isn't there, He reserves the prerogative to let you slip
completely out from under His gracious care.

Because Israel continually suppressed the truth, they
developed a lethal attitude of grumbling and rebelling against
God. They were slandering God. They were blaspheming
God. They were libeling God. They were denying the truth
about God. They were twisting the facts because life wasn't
going their way. They were lying, bold-faced, in the face of
the evidence and facts, and continued the lie.

There is a distinction between complaining about God
and bringing concerns and fears to God. As Christians, we
can become discouraged and experience disappointments
and setbacks. When those things occur, we should bring our
complaints *to God*. There is a way to complain correctly.

Think about your own children and how you deal with
their disappointments. If you let your children whine, they
will develop a spirit of entitlement and have a set of demands.
They will have a sour attitude and a complaining heart that
is pure selfishness. That is sin, and you should recognize it as
such and deal with it.

But there is another kind of complaint that your children can bring to you with a completely different spirit. They are in trouble, they are in difficulty, and they want to tell you about it. They are frightened or anxious or troubled deep in their hearts. And you want to hear their concerns and struggles because they are coming with the right heart.

There is a right kind of complaint and there is a right way to bring it to the Father.

COMPLAINING CORRECTLY

Complaining *to* God is totally different from complaining *about* God. And there is a way to complain correctly, even when you're in the wilderness, and it all has to do with the attitude of your heart—whether it's bent on striking out against the Lord or acknowledging Him and submitting to His gracious ways.

Consider again the words of Paul, this time from Philippians.

> Be anxious for nothing, but in everything by prayer and supplication with thanksgiving let your requests be made known to God. And the peace of God, which surpasses all comprehension, will guard your hearts and your minds in Christ Jesus. (4:6–7)

That's correctly complaining. And it has several components that make it an honorable way to approach God with a concern.

First, *complain in prayer.* Bringing your complaints to God means you're acknowledging Him as worthy and able. That's what prayer really is: acknowledging the Lord, not accusing Him.

Second, *complain in praise.* Praise God because you're thankful. Bitter and angry hearts don't offer praise to God. Only thankful hearts offer praise because they have the right perspective in the midst of their difficulties. Paul exhorted believers to bring everything to the Lord in prayer, *with thanksgiving.* It was John Calvin who observed, "We have short memories in magnifying God's grace. Every blessing that God confers upon us perishes through our carelessness, if we are not prompt and active in giving thanks."[8]

David showed us how this looks in Psalm 100:

> Shout joyfully to the LORD, all the earth.
> Serve the LORD with gladness;
> Come before Him with joyful singing.
> Know that the LORD Himself is God;
> It is He who has made us, and not we ourselves;
> We are His people and the sheep of His pasture.
> Enter His gates with thanksgiving
> And His courts with praise. (vv. 1–4)

Come to God, acknowledging that we are not God and He is. We have life because He gave us life. We breathe because He lets us breathe.

What are the greatest accomplishments of your life?

Whatever your accomplishments—your work, your education, your family, your athletic prowess—they all come from God. Come to Him with thanksgiving and let your concerns be made known to Him. Because He is God.

I always marvel and shutter at the same time while watching professional football players, especially young receivers. I've watched as almost miraculously a guy catches a football in the end zone, then goes into his celebratory dance. Actually, he didn't catch the ball. It went through his hands and lodged in his face mask, but both of his feet were in, so in the NFL, it's a touchdown! Plus, he dropped the previous five. But as that ball is lodged in his face mask, it's time to celebrate. "I'm great," he declares.

The point is, he's not great. The God who made him is great. You're not great either. On the rare occasion when you catch a ball, it's because you've been given hand-eye coordination by God and the ability to concentrate.

First Corinthians 4:7 states it best: "What do you have that you did not receive? If then you received it, why do you boast as if you did not receive it?" (ESV).

Here's the point: it all comes from God. He made you. He deserves the thanks, even in the wilderness when your life is breaking apart. It's okay to complain to God, but bring your worries to Him with thanksgiving and with an awareness of who He is. And while you are thanking Him, be sure to thank Him for the next breath that you will take. It's a well-timed help from His grace (Acts 17:25).

Third, *complain based on truth*. As we approach God in

prayer and bring Him concerns or complaints, those responses need to be rooted in the truth of His Word.

Again Psalm 100 helps us: "It is He who has made us, and not we ourselves. . . . For the LORD is good; His lovingkindness is everlasting and His faithfulness to all generations" (vv. 3, 5).

Now, that's a great perspective for us to have as we bring our complaints to God. He is the maker. He is good. And His faithfulness has been undeniable from eternity past. That kind of laser truth cuts through the fog of our bad attitude and brings about a new and God-honoring perspective.

He was faithful to those people coming out of Egypt, and they still denied His faithfulness in the desert. They had lost perspective. You can't do that. I can't do it. Yet when things do happen to us, it's okay to complain correctly because God is able to respond and provide. It's all a matter of attitude.

Fourth, *complain with honesty and humility.* The best example of this in Scripture is from David, Israel's shepherd-king. The guy figured out the balance of being honest with the Lord about his life while at the same time bringing some rather boldly stated requests to Him. Look at Psalm 31, for example:

> In you, O LORD, I have taken refuge;
> Let me never be ashamed;
> In Your righteousness deliver me.
> Incline Your ear to me, rescue me quickly;

Be to me a rock of strength,

A stronghold to save me. (vv. 1–2)

David was clearly in trouble. Something had him by the throat, yet he turned to the Lord, not accusing Him, but affirming all His goodness and faithfulness. And he demonstrated a genuine transparency and humility as he made his bold demands.

David composed half of Psalms, and you often see him coming clean and talking about his life. He stated what he was going through with a refreshing humility. There's nothing wrong with that because he was talking to his Father.

Complaint and praise are intermingled in Psalm 31. But David was not complaining *about* God; he was complaining *to* Him. He was not slandering God. He was not libeling God. He was not blaspheming God. He was not denying the works of God. He was not suppressing the truth about God.

David was in trouble but said to God, "You will pull me out of the net which they have secretly laid for me, for You are my strength" (v. 4). He could have complained about being ensnared in the net of that circumstance, crying out about how unfair God had been. Instead, he humbly acknowledged his situation and affirmed his confidence in the Lord's faithful response.

He was not bitter because he had troubles. He was calling to the Father because he had a perspective that these troubles were a tool God was using in his life to bring about maturity and faith. Now read his final press.

Be gracious to me, O LORD, for I am in distress;
My eye is wasted away from grief, my soul and my
    body also.
For my life is spent with sorrow
And my years with sighing;
My strength has failed because of my iniquity,
And my body has wasted away.
Because of all my adversaries, I have become a
    reproach,
Especially to my neighbors,
And an object of dread to my acquaintances;
Those who see me in the street flee from me.
I am forgotten as a dead man, out of mind;
I am like a broken vessel. (vv. 9–12)

What a perspective. See the difference between complaining *about* God and complaining *to* Him? David was not accusing God; he was running to Him in transparency and humility. He had learned the faithfulness of God, even in the wilderness.

A NEW PERSPECTIVE ON COMPLAINING

Why does God take you through these trials and struggles? Because He is up to something. Because He wants to train you. Because He wants to develop you. Because He wants to mature your faith in Him. David in all his transparent boldness never lost his perspective of giving honor and praise to God. As we have already discussed with David, it's another reminder of the importance of spending time in the Word, because when you read the Word, you get a perspective about what God is doing in your life through adversity that will guard and calibrate your attitude.

God will never allow an affliction if He does not intend to provide greater grace down the road.

Unless there is known sin in your life that you're not dealing with, God is for you. And if there is known sin in your life that you're not dealing with, He will discipline you (Heb. 12:5–13). He's still for you, and because you're His son, He will not allow you to get away with your sin. He's for you—therefore, He will discipline you. Don't you do that with your kids? Of course you do.

That is the perspective that comes to us only from the Word of God. His truth helps us keep our balance and keep our hearts thankful in the midst of hardships. Like David, it guards us from grumbling and murmuring and accusing God in bitterness.

Philippians 1:6 declares that "He who began a good work in you will bring it to completion at the day of Jesus Christ" (ESV). If that's true, wherever you are right now—even in the pain, the difficulty, the hardship, and the confusion—you can praise Him because the Lord *will* accomplish what concerns you. His will for your life cannot be thwarted. You may not be enjoying the wilderness, but you can praise Him for it.

GIVING THANKS FOR THE FLEAS

I recently read again Corrie Ten Boom's amazing autobiography, *The Hiding Place*. Corrie Ten Boom, along with her father and her sister, Betsie, lived in Holland during the Nazi occupation. They took in some Jewish families but were eventually found out and sent to the concentration camps. Her father died, and her sister, Betsie, eventually died too.

During that horrible imprisonment, Corrie and Betsie were imprisoned together. Betsie grew ill and failed physically very quickly. Yet somehow she maintained an amazing perspective on the sovereignty of God based on the promises of Scripture.

When Corrie would get impatient and discouraged, Betsie would say, "Corrie, in everything give thanks [1 Thess. 5:18]. We cannot lose our thankful hearts." Crammed into a dormitory with hundreds of women, they lived in deplorable conditions. The place was completely infested with fleas. In their hair. In their bedding. In their clothes. Even in the food. They couldn't sleep at night without breathing fleas. They couldn't wake up in the morning without swallowing them.

Corrie had managed to keep a small Bible, the only one in the whole place. With fear and trepidation, one night she opened the Bible and invited the women to gather around her to listen to her read. They huddled very quietly, fearing the guards would discover them and punish them severely.

The guards didn't come. The next night they read the Bible again. The guards didn't come. The Bible study went on for weeks without any interference from the guards.

One night Corrie was so discouraged she said, "Betsie, I cannot take these fleas. I can't take another moment with these fleas." Betsie said, "We must be thankful for the fleas." Corrie indignantly replied, "Betsie, I cannot thank God for the fleas."

Betsie replied gently (I am paraphrasing), "Why do you think we have Bible studies without the guards coming in here? Why do you think we're safe to pray? Why is it that we're in this horrible place, yet safe and sound? Because of God's protection. Corrie, it's the fleas. God has sent the fleas. The guards want nothing to do with the fleas. Let us give thanks for the fleas."

At the end of this chapter, would you join me in prayer?

Father, thank You that You work for our good even when we can't perceive it. There are hard things in life. There are things that come in and break our hearts. Betsie died in that concentration camp, but when she died, she was immediately promoted into Your presence. Only the truth of the Word of God can set us free. Encourage our hearts to trust You even in the worst of circumstances.

If we have become hardened, if we have become angry, if we have become bitter, restore to us the joy of our salvation, so that we will be able to recognize the well-timed helps that You give us as coming from Your hand. Thank You for the manna . . . all of it, even the manna that's camouflaged as fleas.

In Jesus' name, we pray.

8

BE MANNA FOR
YOUR KIDS

"You shall teach them diligently to your sons
and shall talk of them when you sit in your
house and when you walk by the way and
when you lie down and when you rise up."

—DEUTERONOMY 6:7

There are lessons for us to be learned from Israel's wilderness wandering and God's provision of manna. Manna was a provision. Manna was providence. The Devil is not in the details of our lives; God is in the details of our lives. When Jesus said He was the Bread of Life, He meant He is our provision for every area of our lives. These are the lessons that we are to learn.

There are three critical truths that we must tattoo on our minds about the lessons we learn in the wilderness.

- *We are to learn these lessons.*
- *We are to teach the lessons to our children and grandchildren.*
- *When we teach the lessons to our children, we actually become manna to them and for them.*

When we teach the lesson as parents and grandparents, we are God's provision to our kids and grandkids to equip them for life. Parents are designed by God to supply well-timed helps to their children.

Have you ever thought of yourself as manna to your sons and daughters, to your grandsons and granddaughters? That's precisely what you are to them.

INSTRUCTIONS TO THE KING

In Deuteronomy 17, the Lord was giving directions for the king of Israel. At this point in history, they didn't have human kings, but they soon would. The king would be responsible for the well-being of the nation and for leading the people in the right path of God. *And the only way he could do that was to consistently read and apply the Word of God to his life, his behavior, and his leadership.*

And when he sits on the throne of his kingdom, he shall write for himself in a book a copy of this law, approved by the Levitical priests. And it shall be with him, and he shall read in it all the days of his life, that he may learn to fear the LORD his God by keeping all the words of this law and these statutes, and doing them, that his heart may not be lifted up above his brothers, and that he may not turn aside from the commandment, either to the right hand or to the left, so that he may continue long in his kingdom, he and his children, in Israel. (vv. 18–20 ESV)

We've heard it said that every parent oversees a small civilization. If you have a family, that's a small civilization. You have your wife and your kids. As the king of Israel gave an account to the Lord for the nation, you will give an account to the Lord for your family. So when you get down to it, God holds you to the same standard that He did with any other king.

One of the daily responsibilities of the king is to feed on the Word of God. The Word of God is our daily manna. In the wilderness, the manna appeared on the ground, but they had to gather it. God didn't serve them breakfast in bed. They had to get up in the morning and gather the food that was right outside their tents.

You may be wondering why we are covering this subject again. It is of such importance that we are going to briefly remind ourselves of the absolute necessity of reading the Scriptures all the days of our lives. And let me shoot straight with you—are you doing that? Or are you just hitting and missing? If you have not developed a consistent time in the Word, consider this a short refresher course that the Enemy wants you to skip over. Don't take the bait.

We live in a country where we have unbelievable access to the Word of God. There are some countries that don't have access to Bibles, where Bibles have to be smuggled in. It is a huge event for someone to hear that there is a Bible in a city. They will trek for hundreds of miles to actually see a Bible, let alone read one. But we have Bibles everywhere. We have multiple Bibles in our homes. You may have a Bible on your phone or your iPad. But it's very easy to go weeks without ever opening your Bible.

I heard a great phrase this week from Os Guinness: the weapons of mass *distraction*. That's brilliant. That's why it is such a battle to consistently be in the Word of God. We're battling against mass distractions that keep us from it.

Dr. Howard Hendricks did a survey many years ago. I remember hearing about it in class. I called him years later and quoted it with his permission in my book *Finishing Strong*. He surveyed 246 pastors, missionaries, and youth workers, all of them men committed to Christ. What did they have in common? They had all fallen into sexual immorality when they were in ministry. He interviewed each one of them and found some traits in their lives.

One of the patterns he found was that they had no

personal time in the Word of God. They used to, but as the years went by, they thought they could get by without feeding daily on the Bible. They couldn't. These guys were all doctrinally sound. They weren't heretics. I went to seminary with a few of these guys. Even though they were in ministry and teaching others, they had pretty much put their Bibles away and were coasting on the knowledge they had accumulated over the years. They were no longer in the Word consistently.

In their early years they would have died for Christ. They would have done anything for Christ. But then they began to think they could skimp on the nourishment of their spiritual lives. Note what Jesus said in Matthew 4:4: "MAN SHALL NOT LIVE ON BREAD ALONE, BUT ON EVERY WORD THAT PROCEEDS OUT OF THE MOUTH OF GOD."

Somehow they quit taking that seriously.

You have to be feeding on the Word of God or you're in trouble. You will become malnourished. You will become sickly. You will not be able to fight the good fight. You won't be able to stand firm. You won't even stand up because you are too weak. Satan will try to dupe you and convince you that you don't need to read the Bible or you don't have time for it.

> Now it shall come about when he sits on the throne of his kingdom, he shall write for himself a copy of this law on a scroll in the presence of the Levitical priests. It shall be with him and he shall read it all the days of his life, that he may learn. (Deut. 17:18–19)

Why should you read the Word all the days of your life? "That he may learn to fear the LORD his God, by carefully observing all the words of this law and these statutes, that his heart may not be lifted up above his countrymen" (vv. 19–20). If your heart is lifted up above your countrymen, you will think, *They are there to serve me, instead of me serving them.* But the Son of Man did not come to be served; the Son of Man came to serve. That's a heart issue.

When someone becomes controlling, when an individual thinks he's the center of the universe, it's all downhill from there. When you think it's all about you, you have heart trouble, as they used to say in the fifties. I can remember my grandpa went to the doctor, and I can remember hearing that he had "heart trouble." We don't use that phrase a lot, but it means you have high calcium or cholesterol or whatever. You have blockage. That's heart trouble.

Well, there's a spiritual heart. What does the Scripture passage quoted above say? He's to read the Word of God all the days of his life that he may learn to fear the Lord his God by carefully observing . . . *carefully observing.* This isn't a five-minute, fly-through-it thing. The Scripture says, "By carefully observing all the words of this law and these statutes, that his heart may not be lifted up."

Christianity is always about the heart. Always. Man looks at the outward appearance; God looks at the heart. David was a man after God's own heart. Deuteronomy 6:5 says, "And you shall love the LORD your God with all your heart." It's important to be in the Word to keep your heart balanced.

That his heart may not be lifted up above his countrymen and that he may not turn aside from the commandment, to the right or the left, so that he and his sons may continue long in his kingdom in the midst of Israel. (Deut. 17:20)

How did the Israelites stay in the Word of God? Gutenberg had not invented the printing press, and they didn't have iPhones, so how did David read God's words? He didn't have access to the completed Word of God, but he did have portions of Scripture. David would have heard the scriptures taught and he would have had access to the books that were written. He would have taken pen in hand and written his own copy of the Word of God.

And then he would have read it every day, because, "MAN SHALL NOT LIVE ON BREAD ALONE, BUT ON EVERY WORD THAT PROCEEDS OUT OF THE MOUTH OF GOD" (Matt. 4:4). David did not treat this lightly, nor should you. It is your life.

Second Timothy 3:16 states, "All Scripture is inspired by God and profitable." You probably spend a lot of time every day trying to make a profit, because you have a family and bills and tuition and taxes to pay. There's nothing wrong with that. Some would disagree with that, but the Bible wouldn't. There's nothing wrong with making a living by hard work, honest work.

"All Scripture is inspired by God and profitable for teaching . . ." Because we need to be taught. ". . . for reproof . . ." Because sometimes we get out of whack. We start to take a wrong step and need to be reproved. When I need to be admonished, the Scripture admonishes me. If you are teachable, that's to your profit. If you're not, you're finished.

He doesn't just reprove us, He corrects us: ". . . for training in righteousness; so that the man of God may be adequate [or, literally, completely furnished], equipped for every good work."

God has a work for us to do. According to Ephesians 2:10, you can't die until you do your work. How are you nurtured to do your work? By the Word of God.

We should learn the lessons from the Word of God and then teach those lessons to our children and grandchildren.

But if we are not consistently in the Word, then

- we cannot spiritually lead;
- we cannot teach spiritual truths; and
- we cannot be a spiritual mentor who provides manna.

That isn't what we want. We want to lead and teach and guide our children and grandchildren with integrity.

Deuteronomy 6 clarifies how we can do the job with the Lord's help.

COMMANDED TO LEAD

Deuteronomy 6 was addressed to the men of Israel. Note the direct words to the fathers and grandfathers:

Now this is the commandment—the statutes and the rules—that the LORD your God commanded me to teach you, that you may do them in the land to which you are going over, to possess it, that you may fear the LORD your God, you and your son and your son's son, by keeping all his statutes and his commandments, which I command you, all the days of your life, and that your days may be long. (vv. 1–2 ESV)

The Lord addressed the men because He has put the responsibility of their homes upon them, and it is a great responsibility. Men are to lead by their words and by their behavior. We will never be perfect, but we are to strive to be consistent. There should be congruency between what we say and do. Our words and our lives should add up and make sense to our children. They should see a congruency in our lives. Something is congruent when all of the pieces fit together. Paul told Timothy to "pay close attention to yourself and to your teaching" (1 Tim. 4:16).

There should be a consistency between your beliefs and your behavior. Model what you teach! When you don't, confess to those you have hurt. That's leadership. It's what the Lord expects.

This is what you desire or you wouldn't be reading this book. But I ask you, how can you play this role in the lives of your family if you are not habitually in the Scriptures? I grant you, this is a struggle. It certainly is for me. But it is necessary for you to be the man and leader you are called to be.

———

I'm thankful the Lord didn't delete from Scripture the story of Israel struggling in the wilderness. He could have hidden the darker, less-impressive portions of Israel's history and only included those episodes when they demonstrated great character and perfect obedience. The problem with that is it doesn't square with life. At least not my life. Probably not yours either.

You and I benefit and learn from harder times. My kids and grandkids need to learn from me when I'm at my best, but they also learn when they watch me struggle. They need to know both sides of my story. And God has given that responsibility to all of us as men.

One of the lessons to be learned is that the Israelites themselves never learned the lessons. And in that, they became a negative model.

Do you know there are two kinds of role models? We all want positive role models and know the benefits of being around people who live their lives in ways we want to emulate. But it is also true that we can learn a heck of a lot from a lousy role model.

You've probably had a good boss at some point in your life. You've probably had a bad boss too. If you're teachable, you learned from both of them. Maybe you had a father who did not care for you or provide for your family. That's a hard reality to overcome because it creates such deep wounds. But there are lessons you can learn from that experience. You are not doomed to repeat the mistakes of your parents. Maybe you feel you didn't have a great role model in your dad. But actually, you did. And the lesson is to do the opposite of what he did. If he neglected your mother, you don't neglect your wife. If he neglected you, you nurture and provide for your children. If he couldn't control his liquor, you control it. In other words, you can learn as much from a negative role model as you can from a positive one.

Whether you had a good role model or a poor one, you must decide what kind of person you will become. It's in your court. By God's grace, you can become the example your family so desperately needs.

The people of Israel were a negative role model, and we can learn a ton of lessons from them. Not only are *we* to learn them, but we are to pass them on to our children and grandchildren. But you cannot do it if you are not consistently in the Scriptures.

If the king of Israel was to make the Word of God a priority all the days of his life, why would we not do the same? It is a battle, but it is a battle that must be fought so that we can lead with integrity.

COMMANDED TO TEACH

Your children and grandchildren have a lot to learn from you, both by hearing about when life was good and when you felt like you were paddling against the current.

In fact, you are under God's command to obey the Lord

and teach your children and grandchildren along the way. Here's what God commanded in Deuteronomy 6:

> Now this is the commandment, the statutes and the judgments which the LORD your God has commanded me to teach you, that you might do them in the land where you are going over to possess it. (v. 1)

God has many lessons He desires for us to learn and then teach to our children.

Teach the Importance of Obedience.

"Now this is the commandment, the statutes and the judgments which the LORD your God has commanded me to teach you, that you might do them" (Deut. 6:1). Obedience was paramount for God's people.

Eventually they were going to enter into the promised land. So the Lord had certain things that were important for them to learn. Obedience would be critical in the future. And Israel's next generation needed to learn obedience too.

It is one thing to know the Lord's commands; it's another to acknowledge and to *do* them. Isn't that what we want for our kids? We teach our kids, and then there is great joy in our lives when we know our kids actually heard us and they do what we asked them to do. It's an even greater joy when they determine to own their faith in God—to learn the wondrous joy of obedience and trust for themselves.

That's a wonderful thing. But it's a process. It doesn't happen overnight.

Teach the Value of Reverence and Respect.

"So that you and your son and your grandson might fear the LORD your God, to keep all His statutes and His commandments which I command you" (v. 2). Worship would become the centerpiece of Israel's experience with God— not only in the wilderness, but also once they entered the land of promise. From the tabernacle to the temple, God's people would learn the value of fearing Him in all their ways, by keeping His statutes and commands and by acknowledging Him in worship.

How you and I conduct our lives has a greater impact than we may realize. Our sons and daughters must grab from us the importance of living a worship-focused life—of living in fear and reverence for the Lord. And that's a lifelong responsibility.

Sometimes we think our responsibility is to oversee, care, and provide for our immediate families, and that care ends when the children leave the nest. But you're still a parent, even when your kids become adults. It's different, for sure, but you're still commanded to teach. By your words and by your behavior, you are instructing *your* children, but you're also instructing your children so they can raise *their* children.

That reality can feel overwhelming. Don't fret over what you should have or could have done when your children were young. That all may need to stay in the past. We always think about what we didn't do. Nobody bats a thousand as a parent. The heavenly Father alone has that type of average. Nobody else comes close. We've all made a lot of mistakes, so don't sweat it.

What matters now is tomorrow. And the next day, and the next decade, and the end of your days. Hopefully you're growing as you go through life. You're more and more teachable and honest. If you've hurt somebody in your family, go and talk to them. Ask forgiveness. Don't let wounds foul and fester. Take care of it. Don't let it get worse.

Teach your children the value and power of reverence and living your life as worship before the Lord.

Teach the Pursuit of a Lifelong Faithfulness.

"To keep all His statutes and His commandments which I command you, all the days of your life, and that your days may be prolonged" (v. 2). Few things matter more to the Lord than the end game. As we mature (some of us don't really come to our senses until a little later in life), we want what we say we believe and the way we are living to be consistent. We want to develop a lifelong faithfulness. That does not happen overnight.

Here's something I've learned. As a parent, you don't have to be perfect, but you have to be honest. If you have an atmosphere in your home of grace and mercy, appropriate discipline, and respect, if you're mature enough to admit when you mess up, everything is going to be fine. The tone you set for your life will impact your family the rest of their days.

We all go through life with daily opportunities to follow and worship the Lord. My advice to you is to stay teachable and learn the lessons. The people depending on you will be the beneficiaries of your faithfulness. And it needs to be a lifelong faithfulness.

If you do what Deuteronomy 6 says and listen to the commandments, live rightly and humbly before the Lord your God, and teach your children what He has commanded you to teach them, then there's going to be favor in your home. And it won't just accrue to you and to your kids, but it'll go to the next generation.

SETTING AN ULTIMATE COURSE

Psalm 78 is a history of God's people. And its refrains are the clues and details of the ultimate course set by God. There is both the thrill of victory and the agony of defeat. Periods of obedience and worship are interspersed with long stretches of rebellion, followed by judgment and God's ultimate deliverance. It's a revealing pattern for what most of your life will likely look like. Let's look at a brief section of this magnificent psalm.

> Listen, O my people, to my instruction;
> Incline your ears to the words of my mouth.

I will open my mouth in a parable;
I will utter dark sayings of old,
Which we have heard and known,
And our fathers have told us.
We will not conceal them from their children,
But tell to the generation to come the praises of the
     Lord,
And His strength and His wondrous works that He
     has done. (vv. 1–4)

We have seen God work. We have learned about His character and power and glory and wisdom. We have a responsibility now to convey those things to the next generation. That's the overarching lesson of this psalm.

That charge includes the youngest to the oldest. You are to teach your children from the beginning the truth of the living God. That is not the pastor's job or the Sunday school teacher's job. You are to be the primary teacher of the Word, and the reality is that you will be teaching them, whether you mean to or not, by your life, by your words, and by your example.

Last Christmas was a memorable one for our family. It was a white Christmas in Dallas, and those are rare. We were all gathered in our front room on Christmas morning: my mother, my wife, Mary, my daughter, my two sons and their spouses, and our first grandchild. Another member of the family was also present: my maternal grandfather, Harry Brown. He died over fifty years ago, but he was represented by a book of poetry he had written and bound with his own hands when he was a young man. The poems were all about the kingdom of God, the gift of Christ, and the power of the Scriptures.

That morning we read the Christmas story from Luke and then my son Josh read some poems my grandfather had written about the Lord nearly a hundred years before. Each family member wanted to hold that book. They wanted to see the classic penmanship on the pages that were written by our forefather.

It was a Psalm 78 moment. Through his book of poetry about the living God, my grandfather was teaching the next four generations about the Lord Jesus Christ on a white Christmas morning.

That's where Israel failed (read the remaining verses of Psalm 78). They refused to submit and chose to grumble against the Lord. And not only did *they* not learn the lessons, they did not pass them on to their kids so their kids could learn them and equip *their* kids.

Thankfully, God is faithful, and it's never too late to do the right thing. There is a course you can follow that promises God's favor and His remarkable blessing not only for you and your family but also on to the next generation. So let's take a closer look at how this works. And we'll let Deuteronomy 6 again guide us.

Love God Deeply.

"You shall love the LORD your God with all your heart and with all your soul and with all your might" (Deut. 6:5). Fathers are to love God deeply. You don't love God 30 or 60 or 75 percent. You love Him with *your whole life.* That's 100 percent.

How do you do that? I have a saying: "Get all in with Jesus." Get in the boat. Quit messing around. Don't have one foot in and one foot out. That confuses kids. If you talk one thing and live another, you're going to confuse them. Be who you are everywhere you are. Your kids and your grandkids are watching and learning from your life.

If you consistently and easily trade going to church on Sundays for being at the soccer games or relaxing at the lake, your kids are going to see that. And then guess what? They'll make those same choices. They'll ditch church for just about anything too.

My neighbor, Rick Wilson, was a defensive coach for the Stars for a long time, and he had a significant ministry in my life. He was always giving me free tickets. So I was at a Stars game one night with one of my sons. Near the end of the first period, I got hungry and headed to concessions. On my way I ran into a guy I had known from Bible study. He looked shocked to see me, and I realized he was holding—and trying nervously to conceal—a bottle of beer.

I had never talked to him about drinking beer. But for some reason his knee-jerk reaction was to hide it. He was nervous and uncomfortable. Do you know why he was so uncomfortable? It wasn't because of *my* conviction about alcohol. He doesn't even know my views on the subject. He was embarrassed because of *his* conviction. He was violating his own beliefs about drinking alcohol.

If you do that consistently, if you say one thing and do another, you're going to send mixed messages to your children, and that's not good teaching. Get all in. Love God deeply. With everything and all that you are. Your kids will get that, and it will set them on a course for lifelong integrity and devotion to Christ.

Be with Them Consistently.

"You shall teach them diligently to your sons and shall talk of them when you sit in your house and when you walk by the way and when you lie down and when you rise up" (Deut. 6:7).

You can't teach your kids if you're never around them. You must commit to be with them consistently. Not all the time; they need their space. But spend time with them consistently. That's what God means by "when you sit in your house and when you walk by the way and when you lie down and when you rise up." You need to be there in the everyday experiences of your kids' lives. And when you are there, you will teach them with your words, with your habits, with your disciplines, and with your life.

I like sitting in my house. I like watching sports. When my kids were growing up, we watched a lot of sports together. After they had their own homes, I got the DirecTV Sunday Ticket so we could watch every pro football game in America. I paid extra for that because it was worth it to me to have something we could all enjoy watching together. I got every college game on satellite too.

I'd often get calls from one of my kids, asking if I got a certain game on satellite. I'd answer, "I get everything."

Here's how the conversation developed. Almost routine.

Josh: "Hey, can I come over?"
Me: "Yeah, come on over."
Josh: "Can I bring Cleve with me? Can I bring John too?"
Me: "I don't care who you bring. Just come on over."

I was always up for it. Do you know why? Because I want to *be with them*. I want to be with my kids so I can teach them. Josh and his friends would come over and we'd watch the game—together. We didn't break open our Bibles at halftime and turn to Romans 9. We just watched the game and hung out. But here's what's cool. Oftentimes when you're with your kids, issues will come up. And then you have the opportunity to deliver truth.

The key word in fathering is *with*. That means being there consistently. In the evenings, on the weekends, for the ballgames, at the school plays, during the rough times, in the good times.

If you're never with your children, you're never going to be able to teach the lessons. The model for parenting and teaching lessons was Jesus with the Twelve. Jesus was always with those men. If Jesus went to Capernaum, they went with Him. If He went to Jerusalem, they went with Him. If He went across the Sea of Galilee, they went with Him.

They were always asking Him stupid questions, just like little kids do. He never treated them like they were an annoyance. What did He do? He listened, and He taught them lessons.

But in order to teach, you have to *be with*. If you have kids, you have a lot on your plate. Use your time wisely. Use your discretionary time very wisely. As much as you can, *be with*, because when you're with, things are going to come up and life is going to happen. You will be able to teach the lessons God is teaching you.

How do you teach? As you're just walking through life. As you're sitting in your house watching a game, a commercial comes on and it's some weird thing. "Man, can you believe that?" the kid will say. All of a sudden you're in a conversation. Then they might ask you a question. Then you're into something, and you're able to convey the truth you've learned. You say, "Guys, I had to learn this the hard way," and they're all ears. They're watching you, and they're listening, and you have them.

You never know when a teachable moment is going to show up. As much as we can, we want to be with our children so that when those moments come, we will be there and ready.

James Carroll wrote, "The curse of fatherhood is distance, and the good fathers spend their lives trying to overcome it."[1] Don't lay a big guilt trip on yourself. Just be aware of it. If there's distance, close the gap. Your time and wisdom will be manna for your kids and for their kids, and on and on it will go.

Actually, by God's grace, you can be the manna for your kids.

Maybe even on a white Christmas day for the generations to come.

9

CONSIDER THE
WORK OF GOD

"The LORD gave and the LORD has taken away,
Blessed be the name of the LORD."

—JOB 1:21

Have you ever been sick with worry? So have I.

Everything that concerns us concerns the Lord, the Maker of the heavens and the earth. He is not silent. He is not indifferent to you or your circumstances. But He does care deeply about how you view Him. He wants you to acknowledge Him and obey His Word and embrace His gracious will for you—even in the wilderness.

There are plenty of things that can get you distracted and

even anxious about your life. The tumultuous economy. The uncertain political climate. Maybe the future of your kids or grandkids.

Add to that, no matter what you do in your business nothing seems to get you above the waterline. You're fighting alligators with everything you've got and you still can't break through the wall. You might even be facing bankruptcy or looking at an ominous physical diagnosis.

That's a lot for a man to manage. You're in the wilderness.

Is there any antidote to that? Actually, there is. "Consider the work of God" (Eccl. 7:13).

Ultimately, the Lord is behind it all. If you don't believe that, I suggest you start reading your Bible carefully from cover to cover. There's manna on every page for you and whatever it is that concerns you. But there's a particular passage in the Old Testament I want to draw your attention to. It's from Ecclesiastes and the heart and pen of Solomon.

> Consider the work of God,
> For who is able to straighten what he has bent?
> In the day of prosperity be happy,
> But in the day of adversity consider—
> God has made the one as well as the other
> So that man will not discover anything that will be
>   after him. (vv. 13–14)

You can't watch cable news for very long before you realize the world is a political and social mess. It's chaos out there. And all of that unrest fuels fears and uncertainties that ultimately impact our personal lives. It's easy to wring our hands and shrink back in fear. But the Bible declares that the Lord raises up nations and sets them down. He has a plan for the ages; it is on schedule to the nanosecond. There are wars and atrocities in every corner of the world. Rumors of wars abound. But in light of the promises of God's Word, you and I need to calm down. And we find peace by knowing and acknowledging who God is. That's what it means to consider the works of God—especially in the wilderness, when everything is coming unglued.

I want to offer you five principles to help you consider how God may be working in your life, whether you're feeling the wind at your back or it feels like you're flying against a headwind. These principles, I hope, will help with both.

GOD OVERSEES YOUR PROSPERITY

"Consider the work of God, for who is able to straighten what he has bent? In the day of prosperity be happy" (Eccl. 7:13). Prosperity comes from God. You might be the one working or building your business, but it is God who causes you to prosper. That's His work. Are you an engineer? Where did you get the ability to be a mechanical engineer? How did you ever pass those courses? He gave you the ability. He gave you the aptitude.

Deuteronomy 8:18 states it plainly: "It is He who is giving you power to make wealth."

Are you a plumber or an electrician? God has provided that skill for you. In our day and age, trades are devalued, but that is honorable work. Jesus worked in the trades most of His life. Those skills are manna for you in order to make a living.

We may not think plumbers are important until we need a plumber. Live long enough in the house you're in and you're going to need a plumber. Not everyone can be a plumber. You have to be wired a certain way to be a plumber. You have to understand certain things. Not everyone can be an electrician . . . and *live*. You have to understand certain things.

Perhaps you make your living selling real estate. You have to enjoy working with all kinds of people to be a successful Realtor. Those are gifts and abilities that come from the Lord. Where did you learn how to deal with people? The Lord gave you the gifts to make a living. Consider the work of God in your life and give Him glory for that work.

He oversees your prosperity. Americans love prosperity. We want as much of it as we can get. We want it to be consistent. We want it to be uninterrupted. But God often allows that to go away in order to break our dependence of material things. But His gracious will is to bless us with abundance when we trust Him.

God told Israel as He described the prosperity of the promised land:

> And when the LORD your God brings you into the land
> that he swore to your fathers, to Abraham, to Isaac, and
> to Jacob, to give you—with great and good cities that you
> did not build, and houses full of all good things that you
> did not fill, and cisterns that you did not dig, and vine-
> yards and olive trees that you did not plant—and when
> you eat and are full, then take care lest you forget the
> LORD, who brought you out of the land of Egypt, out of
> the house of slavery. (Deut. 6:10–12 ESV)

But He also warned against settling into long periods of uninterrupted prosperity. It can turn our hearts. We can be so busy enjoying the ease we forget the One who provided it in the first place. Sometimes the Lord has to regain our attention. He does that through adversity.

GOD OVERSEES THE ADVERSITY OF YOUR LIFE

"In the day of adversity consider: God has made the one as well as the other" (Eccl. 7:14). Most of this book has been about thinking through how best to respond when all supply lines are cut off. When we find ourselves in the wilderness completely at the end of our means, God is there, overseeing the adversity of our lives.

Not too long ago I spoke with a man between services at our church. He and his wife were in their early seventies, and they had lost everything financially. Everything! Now, who would want to be in that position at any point in life, let alone in the twilight years? Yet the more I talked to this man, the more it became obvious he was grounded in the promises of God on His Word. He knew the Word. He trusted the God of the Word. It got him through. He knew God was in his wilderness.

If you know the Word of God, you understand that when adversity comes, ultimately God is behind it. Sometimes trouble comes like a flash flood, without warning. A wife leaves. We lose our job. We get a scary diagnosis. These things happen every day to good people who never dreamed something bad would happen to them.

The response is usually fear. And at times, bitterness toward God. And we're tempted to shake our fists at God and declare, "I didn't sign up for this!" We have plans and dreams for each phase of our lives and our children's lives that we rarely consult God about. You and I tend to live like He owes us prosperity and blessing. We'd love for Him to bless our plans, but rarely do we bother to inquire of Him as to what His plan might be.

God doesn't want spoiled children any more than you do. There is something about adversity that teaches patience, character, obedience, humility, and trust. Children need to fall down every once in a while to learn that they can't do everything on their own. Those are hard lessons to learn.

I have a little granddaughter named Madeleine who is a year old. We have four brick stairs that lead from our living room to our dining room. Madeleine is able now to climb those four stairs. The other day, all the adults present—her mother, her grandmother, and her great-grandmother, and I—were watching her make the attempt. I was up sitting on the stairs and the ladies were behind her as she climbed. She would climb a stair, then turn around, make sure everyone was looking at her, and smile. They would say, "Oh, that's so good, Madeleine!"

Then she would climb the next stair. Then the next. Then the next. All the way to the top. She loved climbing those stairs. But then she wanted to go back down headfirst. That's not the way you go down stairs. I would grab her little arm to keep her from tumbling down.

Well, little Madeleine had a plan for her life and those stairs, and it didn't include me or her mother or her grand-mother or her great-grandmother. It was all about Madeleine. She wanted to go down those stairs. She had her mind made up. As I took her arm to keep her from things she knew nothing about, she resisted because she didn't have an ink-ling of what could happen to her if I let her go her own way. So I just reached out and grabbed her arm.

You and I can act like that, can't we? And sometimes God needs to grab my arm because He knows that left to my own devices, I'm going to crash and burn. If I continue in my stubborn refusal to acknowledge Him, then He may let me fall. That's His prerogative.

It is a blessing of God when He interrupts our plans with a storm. It is a blessing of God when He doesn't give us the dreams we think are so important. It's the only way we can learn life's most important lessons.

GOD OVERSEES THE DISAPPOINTMENTS OF YOUR LIFE

The problem with dreams is they often don't work out as we envision them. Life happens. Things change. Circumstances occur beyond our control. Dreams don't work out as we planned. When that happens, we can feel shocked and stunned.

I can't tell you how often I receive e-mails from men whose marriages are on thin ice. These guys can hardly put two sentences together because they are in such a state of shock. Maybe that's you, or a family member, or someone you know. You've been there, I know.

We still live with this strange illusion that bad things won't happen to good people. But they do. All the time. And at times, without warning. The shock sets in because this twist in life wasn't in the dream. It wasn't part of the plan. But there is a perspective during those times that is critical for you and me to learn. We must consider the work of God. Here's another biblical point of view, this time from the prophet Jeremiah in the book of Lamentations.

My soul has been rejected from peace;
I have forgotten happiness.

So I say, "My strength has perished,
And so has my hope from the LORD."
Remember my affliction and my wandering, the
    wormwood and bitterness.
Surely my soul remembers
And is bowed down within me. (3:17–20)

Those are the words of a man who was feeling the full weight of adversity. He had hit rock bottom. Maybe you are there too. If you aren't, then someday you might be. It's important you consider the work of God and try to understand His mysterious ways. He oversees your adversity, your affliction, and your wandering.

The writer of Lamentations was Jeremiah, the prophet to Israel during one of her darkest periods of rebellion. They called him the weeping prophet because he was maligned, ignored, marginalized, and rejected, all because he obeyed the Lord. And so at one of the lowest points in his ministry, he wrote Lamentations. And confessed he was as down as he could be.

Until . . . *he considered the work of God.* He brought to mind the truths of who God is and how He works. Maybe he read the Scriptures. Perhaps he had memorized something from the Law of Moses. Whatever he did to remind him of the Lord's character turned him from despair to hope. Lamentations 3:21–26 says,

This I recall to my mind,
Therefore I have hope.

The LORD's lovingkindnesses indeed never cease,
For His compassions never fail.
They are new every morning;
Great is Your faithfulness.
"The LORD is my portion," says my soul.
"Therefore I have hope in Him."
The LORD is good to those who wait for Him,
To the person who seeks Him.
It is good that he waits silently
For the salvation of the LORD.

In the middle of adversity, learn to think about the work of God—to consider and reflect on His Word, to acknowledge He is at work. To remember that He has a plan. To trust that He is worth waiting on and pursuing, especially in the wilderness.

When was the last time you fell on your face and called on the Lord, asking Him to give you faith to trust His purpose and plan, to seek His wisdom and gain a perspective on your circumstances that only He could provide? That's what it means to wait on Him. That's what it means to consider the work of God.

When Jeremiah did that, though in absolute despair, he went from wallowing in sadness to feeling a sense of genuine hope.

In the wilderness of despair, I need fresh truth. When I start thinking correctly, I'm going to get my hope back. Jeremiah reflected on the lovingkindness and mercies of the Lord, and it brought him hope. God knows the pressure you're under. In fact, in Lamentations 3:37, Jeremiah declared the Lord has actually ordained it for you: "Who is there who speaks and it comes to pass, unless the Lord has commanded it?"

Whatever you are facing in the wilderness, it could not be in your life unless God was in charge. You don't know what God has planned. All you and I see is the storm. But you can remember that God has a plan and He is in complete charge.

GOD OVERSEES YOUR SPIRITUAL HEALTH

He wants us to grow healthy spiritually just like we want to grow and stay healthy physically. My cardiologist is concerned with the health of my heart. He goes to great lengths to ensure I am healthy and strong. But the Lord is concerned about my spiritual heart. He is the Great Physician named Jesus who oversees my spiritual health. Thomas Watson wrote these words four hundred years ago:

> God is a skillful physician. He knows what is best. God observes the different temperaments of men and knows what will work most effectually. Some are of a more sweet disposition and are drawn by mercy. Others are more rugged and knotty pieces; these God deals with in a more forcible way. Some things are kept in sugar, some in brine. God does not deal alike with all; he has trials for

the strong and [mercies] for the weak. God is a faithful physician, and therefore will turn all to the best. If God does not give you that which you like, he will give you that which you need.

A physician does not so much study to please the taste of the patient as to cure his disease. We complain that very sore trials lie upon us; let us remember God is our physician, therefore he labors rather to heal us than humor us. God's dealings with his children, though they are sharp, yet they are safe and in order to cure.[1]

Whatever your wilderness, God is there, and He is about making sure you grow deeper in your devotion to Him and in your knowledge of His ways. Consider the work of God.

GOD OVERSEES THE PAINFUL SURGERIES OF LIFE

The Old Testament contains the story of Job. Having lost everything, Job remained firm in his confidence in the Lord. The extent to which the Lord allowed Satan to surgically remove things from Job's life is absolutely shocking. Yet Job was undaunted in his resolve. He exclaimed, "Even today my complaint is rebellion; His hand is heavy despite my groaning. Oh that I knew where I might find Him, that I might come to His seat!" (Job 23:2–3).

In the deepest place of his anguish, Job knew God was

there, but he struggled to understand His purposes. And as he considered the work of God, he realized his adversity was the Lord's heavy hand. It was painful, but God was with him. The Lord was doing His work to accomplish His will.

> Behold, I go forward, but he is not there,
> and backward, but I do not perceive him;
> on the left hand when he is working, I do not behold
> him;
> he turns to the right hand, but I do not see him. (Job
> 23:8–9 ESV)

You may feel absolutely in the dark about where you are and why you are in this wilderness. But God has never been in the dark about you. He sees everything in the light. He knows exactly what is happening to you. He knows precisely what you are experiencing. He knows your path. He knows what He is doing and where He is going. He is taking you somewhere.

> But he knows the way that I take;
> when he has tried me, I shall come out as gold. (Job
> 23:10 ESV)

MANNA IN OUR WILDERNESS

I was thirteen years old in 1962. It was a time I'll never forget. It was a year of wilderness that shaped the rest of my life. I didn't realize how significant that year was until a few weeks ago when I was talking with my mother late at night.

We were reminiscing and she said, "Steve, 1962 was such a critical year. You remember the move we made. I always felt that the primary reason God moved us was not just to meet the immediate needs of our family but because He had plans for the future of our boys." God had a plan for me, my brothers, Mike and Jeff, and my family. But none of us could see it at the time.

My family and I were living in Bakersfield, California. My dad was a real estate broker and sold whole subdivisions. That year the market tanked just as he was expanding his business. There was no work, and there was no opportunity. Nobody was buying. There had been prosperous years, but now it was suffocating adversity.

My parents had three boys, ages thirteen, eleven, and nine at the time. Bills were mounting up. My mom and dad didn't know what they were going to do. My parents were under tremendous pressure. They needed a well-timed help, and they could see no possible way of things changing anytime soon. The next Sunday morning my dad got a call from an old army buddy.

Normally we would not have been home at that time on Sunday because we were in church. Like clockwork. That's where we'd be. We were *never* at home on Sunday morning. But the whole family had gotten the flu that weekend so we just happened to be home. Dad's friend was an executive in San Francisco with a savings and loan, and he proceeded to offer him a job, even though they hadn't talked in years. Two weeks later, my dad was working in San Francisco. My mom sold the house, and we moved to a nearby suburb.

Little did I know, that move to a new city would change my life forever. I would enter an immense wilderness I'd never forget.

In Bakersfield, I was the only seventh grader who started on the eighth-grade football team. I was the only seventh grader who started on the eighth-grade basketball team too. Life doesn't get any better than that. And then we moved, and my world came crashing down.

At the new school, the coach cut me in ten minutes from the basketball team because he didn't know me. They put me in the sixth string of football. I didn't even know there were six strings.

My life fell apart. I wasn't popular. I didn't talk like the other kids. I didn't dress like them. Everybody was against me. Junior high is the wilderness for most kids. Also, there was this bully. He didn't like me, so he decided he was going to take me out. He threatened me every day. As I recall, his name was Goliath. He tormented me!

That was the worst year of my life. I had no clue at all that God was in that move. I was just trying to survive.

Can you trust God with your life today, no matter how harsh the wilderness you face? Do you believe He will send you manna for your wilderness? Can you resist the urge with everything in you to take matters into your own hands and instead throw yourself on the mercy of the living God? He will send a well-timed help even though you can't see His manna yet. Can you believe that one day you will look back at this time right now and see the goodness of God?

I have always appreciated the alternative translation of Psalm 46:1 that can be found in the margin of the New American Standard Bible. It reads, "God is our refuge and strength, He is abundantly available for help in tight places."

You may find yourself right now in a tight place. He's not just available to help you—He is *abundantly* available.

Jesus is the Bread of Life.

He's the true manna.

He is God. And He knows how desperate you are for a well-timed help.

Consider the work of God. Help is on the way.

NOTES

Chapter 1: Emergencies and Exigencies

1. *Webster's New World Dictionary*, 3rd College Ed. (Springfield, MA: Webster's, 1988), 444.
2. John Piper, *Future Grace* (Sisters, OR: Multnomah Books, 1995), 294–95.
3. Philip Bennett Power, *The "I Wills" of the Psalms* (Carlisle, PA: The Banner of Truth Trust, 1858, 1985), 2.
4. George Meüller, *Autobiography of George Meüller* (Denton, TX: Westminster Literature Resources, 2003), xiv.
5. Timothy Keller, *Walking with God through Pain and Suffering* (New York: Dutton, 2013), back cover copy.
6. Obadiah Sedgwick, *Providence Handled Practically* (Grand Rapids, MI: Reformation Heritage Books, 2007), 70.
7. John Newton, "Disappointment—What Is Necessary—God's Patience," August 17, 1767, accessed July 15, 2015, http://www.puritansermons.com/newton/Newt_j1.htm.

Chapter 2: Jesus Is the Manna

1. Philip Graham Ryken, *Exodus: Saved for God's Glory* (Wheaton, IL: Crossway, 2005), 428–29.

2. Ibid., 429.
3. Margaret Nicholl Laird with Phil Landrum, *They Called Me Mama* (Chicago: Moody Press, 1975), 82.
4. Don Carson, "Deut. 29; Psalm 119:49–72; Isaiah 56; Matthew 4," *For the Love of God* blog, June 24, 2015, http://www.thegospelcoalition.org/blogs/loveofgod/2013/06/24/deut-29-psalm-119-49-72-isaiah-56-matthew-4/.
5. John Flavel, *The Mystery of Providence* (Carlisle, PA: The Banner of Truth Trust, 1678, 1963), 191.
6. Obadiah Sedgwick, *Providence Handled Practically* (Grand Rapid, MI: Reformation Heritage Books, 2007), 18–19.
7. Abraham Kuyper, "Sphere Sovereignty". In Bratt, James D. *Abraham Kuyper, A Centennial Reader* (Grand Rapids, MI: Eerdmans, 1998), 488.

Chapter 3: Stealth Manna, Stealth Providence

1. Flavel, *The Mystery of Providence*, 15.
2. Westminster Shorter Catechism, cited by J. I. Packer, *Concise Theology* (Carol Stream, IL: Tyndale House Publishers, 1993), 54.
3. Flaval, *The Mystery of Providence*, 16.
4. Thomas Watson, *All Things for Good* (Carlisle, PA: The Banner of Truth Trust, 1663, 1986), 60.
5. Ibid., 61.
6. Watson, *All Things for Good*, 168–69.
7. A. W. Pink, *Gleanings in Exodus*, paperback edition (Grand Rapids, MI: Jay P. Green, Sr., 2002), 123.
8. Ibid.
9. J. I. Packer, *Concise Theology* (Orlando, FL: Foundation for Reform, 1993), 54.
10. Matthew Henry, *An Exposition of All the Books of the Old and New Testaments* (W. Gracie, 1808), 7.

11. Flavel, *The Mystery of Providence*, 85.

Chapter 4: His Time, His Timing

1. Steve Saint, *Walking His Trail* (Carol Stream, IL: SaltRiver, 2007), 66–70.
2. Obadiah Sedgwick, *Providence Handled Practically* (Grand Rapids, MI: Reformation Heritage Books, 2007), 68–69.
3. David Martyn Lloyd-Jones, *Spiritual Depression* (Grand Rapids, MI: William B. Eerdmans Publishing Co., 1965).
4. Ibid., 69.

Chapter 5: Red Leather Chair

1. Tim LaHaye, *How to Study the Bible for Yourself* (Eugene, OR: Harvest House, 2006), 159.
2. Ibid, 159–160.
3. George Gallup Jr. and Jim Castelli , "Americans and the Bible," Bible Review, June 1990, http://members.bib-arch.org/publication .asp?PubID=BSBR&Volume=6&Issue=3&ArticleID=18.
4. Albert Mohler, "Some Thoughts on the Reading Books," albertmohler.com, January 2, 2014, http://www.albertmohler.com/2014/01/02/ some-thoughts-on-the-reading-of-books-2/.
5. You can find some very creative and useful plans online at http://thegospelcoalition.org/blogs/justintaylor/2013/12/26/ how-to-read-the-whole-bible-in-2014/.
6. Ed Stetzer, "BYU Prof Escapes Mormonism," *Christianity Today*, November 6, 2013, http://www.christianitytoday.com/ edstetzer/2013/november/morning-roundup-11613.html.

Chapter 6: Getting Through It

1. Flavel, *The Mystery of Providence*, 127.

2. Ibid., 126–27.
3. Watson, *All Things for Good*, 27.
4. Jon Bloom, *Not by Sight: A Fresh Look at Old Stories of Walking by Faith* (Wheaton, IL: Crossway, 2013), 57.
5. H. C. Leupold, *Exposition of Isaiah, Volumes 1 & 2* (Grand Rapids, MI: Baker Book House, 1968), 475.
6. Augustine, *Confessions*, 2nd ed. (Indianapolis, IN: Hackett Publishing Company, 2006), 55.

Chapter 7: Little Sins

1. Tiffany Owens, "Walking through Fire: Despite Dementia, Elisabeth Elliot Gren Holds Fast to Scripture," *World*, February 21, 2014, http://www.worldmag.com/2014/02/walking_through_fire.
2. C. H. Spurgeon, "Little Sins," The Spurgeon Archive, accessed July 15, 2015, http://www.spurgeon.org/sermons/0248.htm.
3. Ibid.
4. Larry Richards, Ph.D., *The Life of Moses* (Nashville: Thomas Nelson, 2008), 82.
5. Ryken, *Exodus*, 449.
6. Abraham Lincoln, cited by Os Guinness, *A Free People's Suicide* (Downers Grove, IL: IVP, 2012), introductory pages.
7. Flavel, *The Mystery of Providence*, 124.
8. *The New Encyclopedia of Christian Quotations*, compiled by Mark Water (Grand Rapids, MI: Baker Books, 2000), p. 1055.

Chapter 8: Be Manna for Your Kids

1. James Carroll, cited by S. Osherson, *Finding our Fathers: The Unfinished Business of Manhood* (New York: Free Press, 1986), 30.

Chapter 9: Consider the Work of God

1. Watson, *All Things for Good*, 52.

ABOUT THE AUTHOR

Dr. Steve Farrar is the founder and chairman of Men's Leadership Ministries and author of the bestselling book *Point Man: How a Man Can Lead His Family,* as well as fifteen other books. For further information about Steve's ministry, speaking schedule, and online video and audio teachings, please visit his website at: www.stevefarrar.com.